HURTING
AND
HEALING

Thou tellest my wanderings: put thou my tears into thy bottle: are they not in thy book?
(Psalm 56:8)

BY
Patricia R. Williams, D.Min.

Copyright © 2020 by Patricia R. Williams, D.Min.
February 2020

ISBN: 978-1-7344467-2-2

All rights reserved. No part of this publication may be reproduced or transmitted in any form or by any means, electronic or mechanical, including photocopy, recording, or any information storage and retrieval system, without permission from the copyright owner, Patricia R. Williams, in writing, except for fair use.

All Bible quotations are from the Word of God the Authorized Version (the King James Bible).

Published in the United States of America
By
The Old Paths Publications
www.theoldpathspublications.com
TOP@theoldpathspublications.com

CONTENTS

CONTENTS 3
PREFACE 5
CHAPTER ONE: HURT 9
   This chapter evolves from my personal experience and understanding as to why we get hurt.
CHAPTER TWO: REJECTION 17
   This chapter addresses rejection and how we can handle it in a mature fashion
CHAPTER THREE: CRITICISM 43
   This chapter discusses criticism (including its different forms), why it is given, and how we can manage its contents.
CHAPTER FOUR: ROOTS 59
   This chapter reflects upon our upbringing and background and how it plays and intricate role in our relationships and self-confidence.
CHAPTER FIVE: SEPARATION 73
   This chapter involves and in-depth look with regard to separation; it may be attributed to death, divorce, or emotional duress. After our hearts have been filled with pain following separation, the initial healing process begins with the attainment of a humble spirit as we come before God.
CHAPTER SIX: EXPECTATION 97
   We are hurt more by our expectations of others than what others actually do to us. This is attributed to the perfectionist attitude.
CHAPTER SEVEN: FAILURE 109
   This chapter examines failure, which in essence is Faith in reverse. One must learn to not blame others for one's own mistakes or misfortune.
CONCLUSION 117
REFERENCES 119
ABOUT THE AUTHOR 121

PREFACE

Every person who walks through this life will have **HURT** and **PAIN.**

The question is not so much how to avoid hurts, they are inevitable. The question is simply, how do I handle the hurts that come my way in life?

Do I allow these hurts to cause broken relationships or do I overcome them? This little book seeks to point out these matters in illustrations from real life situations so you and I can draw from other sources enough resources and insights to enable us to **overcome.** The words of Jesus are still true,

> *"These things I have spoken unto you, that in me ye might have peace. In the world ye shall have tribulation: but be of good cheer;* ***I have overcome the world****. " (John 16:33).*

HURTING AND HEALING

It Takes The Bitter and The Sweet to Make a Life Full and Complete

Life is a mixture
    of sunshine and rain,

Laughter and teardrops,
    pleasure and pain-

Low tides and high tides,
    mountains and plains,

Triumphs, defeats
    and losses and gains-

But always in all ways
    god's guiding and leading

And He alone knows
    the things we're most needing-

And when He sends sorrow
    or some dreaded affliction,

Be assured that it comes
    with God's kind benediction-

And if we accept it
    as a gift of His love,

We'll be showered with blessings
    from Our Father above.

Helen Steiner Rice, <u>Someone Cares,</u> (Fleming H. Revell Co.) Reprinted with permission.

HURTING AND HEALING

CHAPTER ONE

HURT

Though He Slay Me (Job 13:15)

This chapter evolves from my personal experience and understanding as to why we get hurt.

As I sat in the big overstuffed rocker, my hands felt cold and clammy. I was in a state of shock and shivered incessantly—the chills going through me. It was a hot, 88 degrees in South Florida, yet I sat there, so cold, so numb. As I clutched at an afghan and pulled it around me, my head pounded and I cried desperately. I wanted to pray, but all I could do was repeat over and over, "Oh, God! Oh, God!" I couldn't concentrate on any other words.

It had all started that morning after I had finished making the bed and doing the breakfast dishes. The telephone rang and one of the members of our church needed some information about a meeting that was taking place at the church that evening. We were talking together when the back door opened and my husband, Page, came in. I wondered why he was home so soon. He had just left for work. As I talked, I watched, puzzled, as he locked the back door, then went around closing the drapes. Finally, he

HURTING AND HEALING

motioned for me to end my conversation. Quickly, I excused myself, hurried into the family room, and sat in the rocker, waiting. Obviously, something was dreadfully wrong.

As Page began talking, I suddenly felt sick. He had been under immense emotional stress because of difficulties in the church he was pastoring. *As* he poured out his heart, I discovered the church wasn't the problem. Instead, he said he hadn't been honest with me through the years of our marriage. He began telling me what was wrong with me, how he hated me, and all the appalling things he had done to embarrass me. On and on he went, saying how he felt about me and our marriage. He admitted he had always been afraid of me. It was as though a volcano had erupted. There was no stopping it until all the hot, suppressed, and twisted thoughts and emotions had gushed out.

I couldn't believe what I was hearing. If anyone had asked me, I would have said that we had an "outstanding" marriage. I knew I loved Page, even worshipped him. I believe I would have given my life for him. I had done everything I could think of to make him happy.

I am talented, attractive, and well educated. I could have had a career of my own, but when I married Page, I gave up my desires of having my own business life. My desires were simply to be his wife and to undergird him.

Now, I felt that my whole life was gone. Page was my **life!** By the time he had spewed out the

CHAPTER 1: HURT

venom of his soul, it was close to noon. I began asking Page many questions, trying to find some answers, hoping it was just a grievous nightmare, and wishing I might wake up suddenly and all would be well. I did wake up, but to a reality. I woke up to an awareness that the man I had joined with in "holy wedlock" had not loved me! He had used me to bolster his own ego. My mind began to go back over our life together. Even after remembering about the gruesome headaches I experienced so many times because of his unkind treatment of me (except in front of family and others), I couldn't bring myself to admit that he didn't love me. I'm sure it must have been my "pride" more than anything else that hurt at that moment. Nevertheless, the hurt went deep, deep, cutting caustically into my heart. Even years later, the "scar tissue" lingers in the labyrinth of my mind.

There is an emotional scar tissue similar to physical scar tissue, like when one cuts one's finger. With time, healing takes place, the pain goes away, but the scar remains and is often sensitive to various stimuli. In an emotional hurt, the pain also eventually goes away with the passing of time. However, the scar tissue of the soul remains and is sensitive to what is called, "bad associations."

Communication with Page was very difficult at this point. With considerable struggle, I asked him what he wanted to do. Did he want a divorce? He decisively did not want a divorce. "You are my main stability," he confessed. "Could you help me? Would you help me?" he pleaded. I had mixed emotions, to say the least. He had **hurt** me and I wanted out—out of his life. On the other hand, I did feel sorry for him, so my compassion for him won out.

We began the long road back to recovery. It was necessary for my husband to admit to his emotional instability and lack of self-worth. During this recovery period, my heart deeply HURT. I found myself being supersensitive. Page had been off-base on his assumptions about me and had tried to superimpose his thoughts on me. I felt completely stripped of my personhood. I then began to wonder who I was. I lacked self-confidence for the first time in my life. I had no desire or ambition in any area of my life, except to have a better relationship with God. At the time, we were pastoring a small church, and I felt all the more the criticisms that the people imposed upon me. They did not know what was going on in our personal life. I vowed it would be God and me all the way. I didn't tell my family or any close friends about our troubles. It was God and me.

As Page and I began putting God as the head of our home, we began our relationship over. Page became a new and different man. He became the man I had in mind when I married him. Page's own story about his road to recovery is written and published in a book he wrote, entitled, X-RATED MARRIAGES. (The book is now titled, I DID MYSELF A FAVOR: I LOVED MY WIFE!)

I share this experience with you, not to talk about my marriage. The reader can learn to

CHAPTER 1: HURT

understand why I feel we need to handle **HURT** in a positive way. I feel my hurt has been through death—the death of the man I married and his new life in Christ. I have been through rejection and criticism, separation, and emotional and mental pain. I experienced a broken heart and broken relationships and failure. Thanks be to God, He has taught me how to overcome this hurt and pain. On the following pages, I share with the reader some of my own experiences on this subject. I also tell about experiences of other people with whom I have associated in some aspect of my life.

Many years ago, there was a popular song sung around the country entitled, "What the World Needs Now Is Love, Sweet Love." I agree. The question I keep asking is this, "What is Love?"

God is Love! Without God there is no love. Therefore, if a person does not have a personal relationship with God (not only to believe in, but to live by His Word and by communication with Him through prayer), one CANNOT love. Some people have an intellectual assent to God, but do not have this personal relationship with Him that I am talking about. As the personal relationship with God grows, we become more mature in our love and more understanding of what real love is all about. According to the Bible, love is a command. Jesus says,

> *"These things I command you, that ye love one another" (John 15:17 KJV).*

Today we talk more about "feelings." We say, "I don't feel love." This is true, and yet, this love we are commanded by God to give is more than a feeling. It is a mental attitude. You can choose to love or choose not to love. Most of us are selfish and choose to "be loved." Now, you may ask, what does all of this have to do with **HURT?** Just this; we assume that people love us. They are our parents, they should love us. He is my husband, he should love me. My family is supposed to love me. This is my best friend, he should love me. I believe we are prone to assume that because a person is our relative or friend that he is going to love us. Yet we seldom consider people's "capacity" to love.

If one does not have a personal relationship with God, one cannot love, certainly not the agape (love) which Christ came to demonstrate in His life. He commanded us to do the same. So, it will help us to understand hurt if we begin by realizing that everyone does not know how to love as Christ has commanded. Consequently, even family and friends will hurt us at one time or another, causing us to suffer anguish and pain. People who are jealous of us or uncommunicative to us will inflict a wound on our heart. This will be with less intensity when we realize that it is their problem and not a personality flaw within ourselves.

On the other hand, the problem of hurt may be because of ourselves. Whenever we are touchy and supersensitive, we tend to interpret what another person says or does as a lack of love.

It is necessary for us to learn to manage our hurts if we want our relationships to grow. Growing is PAINFUL.

CHAPTER 1: HURT

The question is not how to avoid hurt, but rather how to neutralize hurt to become our help. The next time you are hurt, begin to analyze it. Check your attitudes about the situation. Why did that person do that to me? Why do I feel hurt? Try to see beyond your situation. Ask yourself, "Am I supersensitive?" This brings to mind the story of the woman whose husband wanted to take her to a football game at his ol' alma mater. She kept telling him that she didn't want to go. Finally, when he insisted that she tell him why, this was her reply: "every time those football players get together in that huddle, I just know they're talking about me."[1]

Now that is what I mean by being supersensitive! It is reading into the words and thoughts and actions of others that are actually not theirs but our own misconstrued thoughts.

If you are not supersensitive, then think about the person who hurt you. Is she *angry* with you, jealous of you, or does she have some personality quirk? As you analyze the situation of your hurt, it is important to pray and ask God's guidance for the right thoughts you should have concerning the hurt. Your prayer might have thoughts like the following:

O, Father in Heaven, my best friend just said some cutting remarks to me. I don't think I have done anything that I know of to cause such

---

[1] S.I. McMillen, M.D., None Of These Diseases (Old Tappan: Fleming H. Revell Company, 1979), p.67.

remarks. If I have, and am unaware of it, then please reveal to me what I have done. If, Father, on the other hand, she has a problem coping with my success and it is her problem, then show me this too. If I am being oversensitive, forgive me and cleanse me. If it is her problem, then teach me how to help her and confront her with the anger she is showing toward me. I choose to forgive her, Father, for these cutting remarks, in the Name of Jesus I pray. Amen.

When these pangs of hurt come your way, the most soothing medicine available is to forgive the person for the hurt. Ask God's forgiveness for your own angry thoughts and ask for God to give you the power to keep your mind off the incident. Many people I have talked with indicate to me that they lay awake all hours of the night thinking of ways to get even, or of what they wished they had said during the situation. But after you have really forgiven, then comes release—release from the information and then the healing of your soul. After reading the following pages of examples of hurt and pain, my prayer IS that you will overcome the hurts in your life and the wounds and broken relationships will be permanently healed.

CHAPTER TWO

REJECTION

Father, Forgive Them for They Know Not What They Do (Luke 23:24 KJV)

This chapter addresses rejection and how we can handle it in a mature fashion.

It was a chilly fall evening, and as I sat next to Page in the car, I was very silent. I was thinking, "I would much rather stay at home tonight than go visiting." Yet, I knew this was important to Page because we were going to visit one of our new deacons. Ted had not been to church in several weeks, and it was unlike him. He was a fairly new Christian and elected to the Board of Deacons just that year. He was very enthusiastic and loved the Lord so much that he brought his entire household to Christ and into the fellowship of the church. Now he had not been to church in weeks, and we were going out to check on him. I stopped thinking and began praying, confessing to God that I'd rather have stayed home, but now that I was on the way, to please let me glorify Him and give Page and me the insight to say the right things.

As we drove into the spacious yard of the beautiful home, Ted was outside working on an old car. He smiled and invited us in to visit.

HURTING AND HEALING

Page got right to the point. He doesn't believe he should delay speaking the truth in love when he is on an assignment for the Lord. "Ted, we've been missing you and your family in church lately, is there anything wrong?" Ted hung his head. "I was hurt and I don't think I can go back to church," he said with an obvious degree of difficulty. Page, realizing that Ted needed to get out his feelings asked, "Would you like to share your feelings with us?"

"Well, it happened about a couple of months ago," he began. "That particular Sunday morning as I was preparing to take up the offering in church, I noticed Sam's new suit, and I commented on it and told him how sharp it looked." (Sam was a financially wealthy member of the congregation.) "Sam and I were serving as ushers. Several weeks later I bought myself a new suit because I was going out of town to a special meeting and decided to splurge. The next Sunday morning when Sam and I met to take up the offering, Sam looked over and noticed that I had on a suit just like his, except mine was a different color. He would not walk down the aisle with me to take up the offering. This created an embarrassing situation. We had to hurry and find another deacon to help take up the offering with me. I was hurt. You see, I had no idea when I bought the suit that it was like Sam's. It simply wasn't on my mind when I was buying the suit. I was definitely hurt—being rejected by another deacon, and especially one who had been a Christian for many more years than me. I never expected this of Sam," he reported as he

CHAPTER 2: REJECTION

shook his head in disbelief.

Without going further with the incident in Tom's life now, and how we can work it out so he and his family can return to the church, I will describe this experience of Tom's as an "illegitimate hurt." Actually, Ted was innocent of any wrongdoing, and yet rejected by his fellow Christian. So, we call it an "illegitimate hurt" when one is the innocent party and has become the victim of a hurt based on another's jealousy or misinformation. One is attacked verbally without the other person knowing all the details of the situation. It never crossed Ted's mind, when he bought his suit, that it would cause such a conflict from a fellow Christian.

Hurt is a universal experience. Only the dead feel no pain. Hurts come in a variety of packages: VOCATIONAL situations, DOMESTIC conflicts, FRIENDS turn of us, NEIGHBORS have untrue opinions of us, CHURCH & SOCIAL transactional hurts, and BROKEN RELATIONSHIPS.

Our daughter, Plythe, had a similar experience when she was beginning her teen years. She and a little friend were close as schoolmates. One day Plythe wore a skirt that I had made for her to wear to school. That day, she also noticed that one of her friends did not speak to her all day long. The next day, Plythe went to school and the friend ignored her again. Finally, on the third day, Plythe confronted her friend. The friend's response was one that really shocked Plythe. The friend said, "You are trying to copy me!" The friend had a skirt just like Plythe's. Now her friend was

HURTING AND HEALING

telling Plythe that she can't wear hers. The reason being because Plythe had already worn the one just like hers. So, talk about innocent. Plythe had no way of knowing her friend owned a skirt "just like hers." Her friend was involved in what we call an "illegitimate hurt." There was no way of Plythe knowing that what she had done in any way inflected pain on another person.

In counseling sessions, we teach people who are experiencing **HURT** that it is not the fact that one is hurt. Rather, it is how one handles the hurt that makes the difference. In the case of the two deacons, Ted and Sam, we tried to show Ted how to forgive his offender, Sam. We taught Ted how to pray and let God know his hurt and to confess it to God. We taught Ted that "forgiveness" is not a feeling. Forgiveness is a decision. It is "letting go of the hurt." Forgiveness is not saying to the person who has wronged you that it is all right or that you are condoning what the person has done. It is simply a decision not to hold on to the hurt or hold a grudge against the person. We encouraged Tom to forgive Sam and to put those hurts behind him.

The Bible shows us what Jesus says,

> *For if ye forgive men their trespasses, your heavenly Father will also forgive you: But if ye forgive not men their trespasses, neither will your Father forgive your trespasses.*
> Matthew 6:14-15

Failure to forgive is like destroying the bridge that you must cross yourself.

CHAPTER 2: REJECTION

Ted's response was that he didn't "feel" forgiveness toward Sam. Page, having received forgiveness when we were having our difficulties in our marriage and having learned to forgive himself, was anxious to explain that forgiveness is not a feeling. It is a decision. You may not feel forgiveness, but you decide to forgive and then the feeling will eventually come. Then Ted asked, "Well, suppose I forgive him and then he won't forgive me?"

"Well, that is what is known as 'unilateral forgiveness'—when you forgive someone and then they won't forgive you," I quickly replied. "This is what Jesus Christ did for us when He died on the Cross and He prayed,

Then said Jesus, Father, forgive them; for they know not what they do. And they parted his raiment, and cast lots. Luke 23:34

I explained, "But you must forgive in order for you to receive the blessings of God's forgiveness of you." Ted then said he was willing to try it because all the Christian principles he had learned so far had not been working for him.

Ted did forgive Sam and went one step further and prayed for Sam. Sam didn't respond immediately to Ted's forgiveness, but when he finally did forgive Ted, they became very good friends. They could even laugh about the "suit incident."

When we feel rejection and hurt, we

HURTING AND HEALING

immediately withhold our flow of love for that person. "If someone hurts me, I will stop loving them. They don't deserve my attention," is the way we might say it.

This is one reason why we have so many broken relationships in the world today; so many people withholding their love and attention. There are some people who are hurt so many times by the same person, you can understand why they won't go back for more. You wouldn't advocate someone putting a finger back on the hot stove after being burned. The Christian life is full of pain and hurt. These hurts are to let us know that we are "alive." These hurts are what make us grow and mature.

There are many people who are bitter and going around holding grudges from many years ago. These same people usually have ulcers, headaches, and all kinds of sicknesses because of their inner emotional turmoil. If only they could confess this to God and forgive, how much happier and healthier they would be.

Page was once counseling me after I came home with a hurt due to what some ladies had said about me. He reminded me that those hurts were to make me grow. He meant spiritually, but I took it literally and replied, "Well, I must be ten feet tall today."

It is important to learn how to handle rejection. There are times when rejection can be good. For example, in our business of counseling

CHAPTER 2: REJECTION

there are times when we cannot counsel with people. It may be for various reasons, but when we tell people we cannot counsel with them, they feel rejection. We try to explain that the Holy Spirit is by far a much better counselor than us. Most people demand the time right now and don't want to go to the effort to pray and get themselves right with God. Also, sometimes these people can become dependent on us rather than on the Holy Spirit. So, in this sense rejection can be good. It is still hard for that person to handle because he wants counseling so badly but it may be the best thing that could ever happen to him.

An example of this happened once when a friend of mine called me one Thursday morning. I was on my way out the door to take my child to the doctor. "Come right away," she cried, "I need you!" I explained that I couldn't, that it was impossible for me. I had a sick child and was taking him to the doctor. It's amazing how selfish people can be when they are hurting. I had to tell her twice that I couldn't, but she didn't want to hear me. She thought she needed me right that moment. I did tell her that I would pray for her, which I definitely did, while I was sitting in the doctor's office.

That evening, as I was getting supper on the table, this same friend phoned. I could tell her excitement in her voice!! She shared with me how when I couldn't come over right away she got so angry with me. She went into a severe state of self-pity. She got so angry that she worked herself into a

HURTING AND HEALING

dreadful headache. The pain from the headache was so bad that she cried out to God to help her. She started talking to Him. Before she knew it, the pain of the trauma that she had been through earlier that morning left her, the headache was gone, and the anger toward me had left her. God revealed to her how selfish she had been in wanting me to talk to her when she should have been wanting to talk with Him instead.

If we are not careful, this is the role many of us counselors get ourselves into; trying to play God. I have found one of the best ways to help people is by teaching them how to have a personal relationship with God. Praying and reading His Word enables one to become dependent on God and not on a counselor. It's amazing how society gets ideas, thinking that the minister is supposed to counsel, regardless of the situation. Years ago, ministers usually met the spiritual needs of the people in caring for the sick and preaching the Word of God. Today, many ministers are allowing themselves to be used as chauffeurs, realtors, job consultants, and baby-sitters. I know of one minister whose parishioner wanted him to hang some wallpaper for her.

It concerns me that some people rely more on the minister than they do on God. I had an experience one Saturday morning. I was working around the house while Page was out officiating at a funeral service. The phone rang.

"Hello," I said.

CHAPTER 2: REJECTION

"Patti, I want to speak to Page!"

"Page isn't here."

"Patti, I want to speak to Page."

"Tommy, Page isn't here," I repeated.

"Well, where is he?"

"He is conducting a funeral," I answered.

"Can you get in touch with him?" he demanded.

"I'll try!" I replied, "what is happening?"

"Mrs. B... just locked herself in her bedroom and fired a shot and she might have killed herself," he gasped.

"Well, Tommy," I replied, "have you called the emergency squad?"

He had not called the emergency squad, so I asked him to hang up and call them. In the meantime, I said I would try to get in touch with Page.

I was able to contact Page and we arrived on the scene not too long after the emergency squad. The lady had not killed herself, but she had blown a hole in the bedroom floor. Right then Page realized that he had been wrong in allowing Tommy the opportunity to grow dependent on him; so much so that Page was the first one he called,

HURTING AND HEALING

even in this situation that called for a different kind of help. Ministers, and others as well, are prone to forget that the minister's priority is to put God first in the minister's own life and then do one's best to share God's insights with them in order to make them capable of being responsible for themselves before God.

As Christians, we must not let people become dependent on us. We must teach them to go to God. This isn't to say that we do not help people. There is always room for helping people, but sometimes the best help we can give, is "no help" at all.

A graphic illustration of this came about some time ago involving an incident with our daughter, Plythe. Plythe was in the tenth grade and was required to take a religion class in her school. Her religion teacher asked all the students to purchase a particular book that they would be using for the remainder of the school year. Plythe got her book and wrote her name on the outside front cover of the book. Her teacher was checking the books to see that all of the students had one. When he saw Plythe's book with her name on the outside, he asked her to put it on the inside instead. As she was leaving her religion class, her friend, Teddy, asked if he could use her book. He had not gotten his yet. In the meantime, Plythe had erased her name from the outside. She wrote it on the inside, as the teacher had instructed her. Teddy, hoping to make the teacher think that he had purchased his book, also wrote his name in the back of the book. The teacher

CHAPTER 2: REJECTION

saw the book and noticed where the name Plythe was erased. He over-reacted. He accused Teddy of stealing the book. He said some real strong and harsh words and threw him out of the class, causing an uproar. Meanwhile, Plythe was in an algebra class down the hall and could hear the religion teacher yelling at someone. She realized who it was when she heard Teddy saying, "but I didn't steal the book!" Soon, the principal came to the class and called for Plythe. Our daughter said that she was terribly embarrassed, felt sick, and a little like she was going to faint. She told the principal and the teacher that she had let Teddy borrow the book. She expressed her gratitude to the teacher for taking up for her. She was hurt that the teacher had made such a scene over the situation and that her friend was fussed at so harshly. She did find out later that some of the other students had not purchased their books. Instead of being honest, and telling the teacher the truth, they lied and said that their books had been stolen. So naturally the teacher was upset when he thought that he had caught one of the thieves. None of this would have happened had Plythe been strong enough to say "no" to Teddy when he asked to borrow her book. Teddy should have been responsible, and since he had not purchased the book, should have been man enough to tell the teacher the truth. So Plythe got hurt unnecessarily because she did something trying to help her friend when "no help" would have been the best help.

So, try to make it a habit of _not_ allowing

HURTING AND HEALING

people to depend entirely on you. I had a friend whose neighbor wanted her and her family to attend their family reunion. My friend explained to them that it would be infeasible for them to go for several reasons. Her neighbor responded to her rejection by saying that she would be hurt if she would not attend the reunion. My friend chose not to attend. As far as I know, to this day, the neighbor still isn't speaking to my friend. This was one of those times that my friend had to choose between being rejected herself, or spoiling her family's priorities.

This situation is not uncommon. I have found times when people get rejected because they refused some invitation. They never heard the end of it. Have you ever felt rejected when someone could not do what you wanted them to do? The maturing person can accept "no" graciously and responds with, "maybe I'll ask again sometime," meaning that they really will ask again if the occasion arises.

Young men often feel rejected when asking girls for dates. My husband did not let "no" stop him. He asked me for a date when I was in the 9th grade and I refused. The next year he asked me again, and again I refused. He asked me for a date for the third time in my eleventh year in high school and I told him that I would let him know later. I finally accepted. I wonder where I would be today had he taken "no" seriously, or as a total rejection.

The next time you feel rejected, ask yourself

CHAPTER 2: REJECTION

the following questions:

1. What have I done?
2. Is this a legitimate rejection?
3. If I have done something wrong, can I explain why I am wrong?
4. Am I innocent?
5. Can I forgive?
6. Can I pray for this person or group?
7. Am I talking with God about this situation?
8. Have I told God that I feel rejected or hurt?
9. Can I put myself in the other person's shoes?

As Jesus hung on the Cross, he pleaded, *"...Father, forgive them; for they know not what they do..."* (Luke 23:34). Stephen, as he was being stoned to death, beseeched, *"Lord, lay not this sin to their charge"* (Acts 7:60).

Most people don't mean to hurt other people. No one gets up in the morning and thinks, "Boy! I am going to have a good day today, I'm going to hurt everyone I meet." Mostly, it is out of selfishness that we do hurt people.

The next time you feel rejected, don't retaliate or try to get even or hold a grudge or become resentful or bitter. Instead, pray and tell God how badly you are hurting. Confess your hurt and anger, forgive the other person, pray for them and ask God to bless them.

HURTING AND HEALING

Remember this Biblical advice:

> *Ye have heard that it hath been said, Thou shalt love thy neighbour, and hate thine enemy. But I say unto you, Love your enemies, bless them that curse you, do good to them that hate you, and pray for them which despitefully use you, and persecute you; That ye may be the children of your Father which is in heaven: for he maketh his sun to rise on the evil and on the good, and sendeth rain on the just and on the unjust .For if ye love them which love you, what reward have ye? do not even the publicans the same? And if ye salute your brethren only, what do ye more than others? do not even the publicans so? Be ye therefore perfect, even as your Father which is in heaven is perfect.* (Matthew 5:43-48)

Remember also to say,

> " *...Father, forgive them; for they know not what they do...*"(Luke 23:34)

The Session of the Presbyterian Church had invited Mrs. Shepherd to come to the meeting to resolve a misunderstanding between her and some of the members of the Session about a decision the Session made concerning a policy in the church. As the meeting progressed, they became aware that Mrs. Shepherd had come there for no such reason. She only wanted to condemn the people on the Session and blow off a bit more steam; so much so that she made a fool of herself in front of the spiritual leaders of the church. She left embarrassed to tears and hurt

CHAPTER 2: REJECTION

because they had invited her there in the first place. She went home and told her husband how dreadfully those men had treated her. They made her go to that dumb meeting. She was never going back to that church again unless every last one of those elders came to her house and personally apologized to her for what they had done to her. Naturally, her husband jumped to her defense and felt she was mistreated. He, too, felt hurt. Someday, Mrs. Shepherd will face the truth and realize that her hurt was self-imposed. She may return to the church ready to live for the Lord, forgive the church officers, and keep on working until the Lord returns. Yet, it is very doubtful that this will ever occur, because she thinks more of her hurt than she does Christ or others. Her hurt is more important to her because it is what she uses to save face and her ego. In our culture, most of us can hide behind our "hurts" and seldom face the truth. Why is this? Because nobody is going to tell you there are various kinds of hurts, some illegitimate and some self-imposed. To tell a person who is hurt that it is self-imposed, is to "hurt" him all the more. This would give him cause never to listen to you again. As long as we let ourselves get by with this self-inflicted hurt to hide behind our ego, we will be in serious trouble personally, socially, emotionally, and worst of all, SPIRITUALLY.

Mrs. Shepherd was going to avoid "those people" from now on. Avoidance is usually a sign of self-imposed hurt, associated with false guilt and a poor self-image.

HURTING AND HEALING

Many people use hurt as an excuse for not doing the things in their life they might normally do. For instance, if someone gets hurt in a church situation, they quit going to church. If a wife gets hurt by her husband, she may dress sloppily. She may not fix herself up. She may overeat and get fat. Some people use hurt to cheat or to get even.

Look at the case of Mrs. Smith. She is a very intelligent, knowledgeable person. Yet, she ran roughshod over her family for years. She was selfish and pursued her own career at the expense of her family. Her husband went his way and she went hers. He felt rejected and defeated because she ran the family and wouldn't allow him to be the man of the home. She was over-involved in church work. One day her teenage daughter ran away and would not come back home. Mrs. Smith almost had a nervous breakdown. She told everyone her problems; so much so that she began losing her friends. People would avoid sitting near her or being with her because she was always talking about her problem. It was always the same song. Susie ran away and she hurt me. "I have done everything in the world I know to change her and make her a fine young woman," she would whine. Mrs. Smith did not change her theme. She would not see her absenteeism from home all those years or her not showing Susie the love and support she needed as a child, as part of the problem. Mrs. Smith just lost herself in her work and in activity after activity to rid herself of Susie's rejection. Her pain was mostly due to pride; pride that her own child could do this to her. She was a

CHAPTER 2: REJECTION

talented mother and they had a lovely home and they were church-going people. How could Susie do this to her? She was so aware of her own pain and hurt that she did not think of the hurt and pain she had inflicted on her own daughter. Through being absent from home all those years, Mrs. Smith gave the impression to her daughter that her job and career were more important than the daughter.

When I talked with Susie, she said her mother usually punished her by making her go to her room and read the Bible. Her mother also made her go to Sunday school and church every Sunday. There were times when Susie was actually sick, and yet her mother made her go to Sunday school anyway. Susie also felt like her mother thought Sunday school (getting a perfect attendance pin) was much more important than she was as her child. When I tried to talk to Susie about God, she kept relating Him to her mother. She said, "I don't feel like I can ever turn to God if He is what makes my mother like she is." Mrs. Smith did not want to talk with her daughter, and she refused to see her. She kept getting busier and busier. She would take her hurt out on her husband, her job, and she even took her hurt out on her church. She blamed her church for the daughter's rebellion. She used her hurt as an excuse for not maturing in her spiritual life and did not look at her own self.

I have seen some people use their hurt to try to control situations as well as other people.

HURTING AND HEALING

Thus, their hurt means more to them than their relationships. Some years ago, during a counseling session, I learned about two sisters. As children, they had a terrible time in their relationship. It was more than the usual sibling rivalry. When they grew older, each married, but the younger sister moved to another state. Over the years while being apart, the relationship survived on sparse letters and a once-a-year visit. Eventually, the younger sister moved back to the same town where her older sister lived. Having grown older, wiser, and walking closer with the Lord, the younger sister decided to do everything she could to have a much better relationship with the older sister. The older sister responded agreeably to the change.

They really worked at their relationship. Their personalities and lifestyles were as different as night and day, yet they managed to be honest and open with each other. One day the older sister came to visit the younger sister and announced that she was getting re-married (having been a widow for five years). The first emotion of the younger sister was shock. The older sister explained that the wedding would take place in her apartment. Her fiance's friend would be standing up with them, and that no one else was invited, including the younger sister. This could have been the setting for a big blow-up, but the younger sister immediately chose not to allow this to hurt her. She gave her older sister the freedom to be who she was by respecting her wishes. Her relationship to her older sister meant more to her than having hurt feelings. So,

CHAPTER 2: REJECTION

she leaned over and hugged her sister and let her know how happy she was for her. A week later, the day of the wedding, the older sister called and was upset because she couldn't get her hair fixed just right. The younger sister jumped in her car, drove six miles to her sister's home, and fixed her hair. She got out of the apartment before the wedding took place.

After the honeymoon, the older sister phoned the younger sister. She expressed her sincere appreciation, especially for the love she felt at the time when she needed it. This is a beautiful illustration that people can change and can chose not to allow others to hurt them. We really can allow people to be who they are without making them feel unloved.

Are there not times when you want to do something without asking certain friends or relatives or neighbors? You want them to respect your freedom, without getting hurt or never speaking to you again. The principle is this: allow people to have their own freedom, as you want yours, without judging. Jesus put it this way:

> *Therefore all things whatsoever ye would that men should do to you, do ye even so to them: for this is the law and the prophets.* (Matthew 7:12)

It is to make a conscious decision to try not to be in control of everyone and everything. When people don't want to do something, then honor their decision, such as when parents expect their

HURTING AND HEALING

married children to remember their anniversary, or when married children don't write home, or acknowledge gifts with "thank-you" notes.

Some people choose to hurt when these social niceties are not completed. Someone may say, "How crude; they are not using the social graces taught to them." This is true. However, if the child or person chooses not to write or send a card, the parent or other person has the power to choose to honor the relationship above whatever hurt he may feel. Although the reasons for not writing the "thank-you" note may be flimsy, maybe they forgot, didn't want to take the time, or didn't have enough money, one still has the choice "to hurt or not to hurt."

The hurt that comes to us by rejection is a very strong feeling. It comes in a variety of packages. Family life is one of those packages in particular where rejection is felt so sharply. For example, a wife feels rejection when her husband does not have time for her. Children feel rejection when parents don't give them quality time. When parents and teenagers are trying to communicate and the teenagers walk away and rebel, the parents feel rejection.

I can remember counseling with a disturbed mother whose son had run away from home. The pain from the rejection she experienced from the runaway son was consuming her whole thought process. I was saying to her, "I understand." But the mother bitterly cried, "How could you understand? You've never had a child run away!" I simply stated,

CHAPTER 2: REJECTION

"You're right, I have not had a son run away, but I have positively experienced the pain of rejection." What I'm saying is simply this, pain in any package has about the same intensity.

ALWAYS KEEP IN MIND, NO PAIN IS GREATER THAN THE MIGHTY GRACE OF GOD!

Another form of rejection some people experience other than from individuals, is with institutions, places of business, credit companies or other groups. I remember when our son was rejected from a medical school in Florida. I was very hurt and humiliated. My prayer about the situation with the school went like this: "Father, I thank you for helping my son Perry in his admission to the medical school so he can be close by. But mainly so he can be eligible for large scholarships, grants and loans that will help us financially with this enormous expense." All of the signs looked good from our viewpoint that God was going to let Perry go to this medical school. He had an excellent interview with the Dean of Admissions. His scores from the necessary tests were high. He had an excellent grade point average, and besides all of that, he had been awarded two scholarships that would have paid his entire expense, if he were accepted. Though there were only four places available in this school for transfer students and over a hundred and fifty students had applied, we nevertheless felt that Perry had an inside track. But, guess what? He did not make it. I was so angry with God. "That's my son, he's good and you should have helped him into that school," I told

God. I was so sure that it was God's will for Perry to go to that medical school! Every time the phone rang, I knew it was them calling to say he was in after all. I finally cried out to God in my desperation. I became preoccupied with my hurt. I began thumbing through the book of Psalms. That is where I always go when I feel desperate. My eyes came to rest on the fourth verse of Psalm 37: "Delight thyself also in the LORD; and he shall give thee the desires of thine heart." Those words just jumped out at me. At that moment, I realized that my desire was not for our son to be in that particular medical school. It was for him to be in God's perfect will. God had something better for Perry. Within a few months, Perry was happily enrolled in another medical school. My relief from pain and hurt came as a result of God's Holy Spirit speaking to me through the written Word of God. I had been praying but had not been asking for God's will. It was my selfish desire from my own point of view. I was just telling God what I wanted, or what I thought I wanted. As His Word spoke to me, I realized I wanted only God's will in our son's life. Then glorious peace filled my heart.

I BELIEVE THAT THE ANSWER TO OUR PRAYERS IS NOT IN GETTING WHAT WE ASK FOR. IT IS IN THE RECEIVING OF THE PEACE IN OUR HEARTS THAT PASSES ALL UNDERSTANDING.

Paraphrasing the Apostle Paul, He put it this way: Don't worry about anything, instead, pray about everything, tell God your needs and don't forget to thank him for his answers. If you do this

CHAPTER 2: REJECTION

you will experience God's peace, which is far more wonderful than the human mind can understand. His peace will keep your thoughts and your hearts quiet and at rest as you trust in Christ Jesus.

> *Be careful for nothing; but in every thing by prayer and supplication with thanksgiving let your requests be made known unto God. And the peace of God, which passeth all understanding, shall keep your hearts and minds through Christ Jesus.* (Philippians 4:6-7)

Many times, we hurt people when we are pre-occupied, or not listening to what's going on. Have you ever been making a statement and realized that the person is looking around and putting his attention on someone else or something else in the room? There is a feeling of rejection. Perhaps he wasn't very interested, or he wasn't listening to you very well in the first place.

I was on a committee of an organization some years ago. The committee had met to elect a new chairperson and to begin work on the new projects for the year. The president of the organization had met with our committee to challenge us and to make a few remarks of encouragement. One strong point he brought out was the importance of electing someone new and different to serve as the committee chairperson. This was to give more people the opportunity to serve and to be trained. The president sat down, and the committee then proceeded to elect a chairperson. The floor was opened for nominations. "I nominate Mr. Brown," said a young man on the committee. The young

HURTING AND HEALING

man and everyone in the room was aware that Mr. Brown had already served as chairperson on previous occasions. Mr. Brown replied, "No, I believe we need to get someone new." But as the business session went on, Mr. Brown was finally elected as chairperson of that committee.

After the meeting, I was wondering how the president must have felt. I was thinking that the young man was simply defying what the president requested. But as I talked with the president, he said that the young man did not even hear his opening comments. He had known the young man for a few years—his occupation was a dentist. As a dentist, he had trained himself to talk to people, but not to listen. When the dentist worked on patient's teeth he talked. The patient could not talk back with all those gadgets in his mouth. So, the dentist had set up a pattern of not listening. The president had seen this young dentist in other groups, whispering while someone else was talking, or preoccupied in his mind. The president's wife was a school teacher and had contact with the dentist's children. The children complained, "Daddy does all the talking and won't listen to us." So the dentist was hurting many people, his children, his friends, his club members, all because he did not LISTEN.

There are many expressions such as: "Do you know what I mean?"; "Are you listening?"; Are you there?"; "What did I say?"; and "Do you understand me?", which I hear from people almost everywhere I travel across the country. This tells me that this could very well be a "universal"

CHAPTER 2: REJECTION

problem—this feeling of rejection, because others do not seem to be listening. It hurts. This problem seems to be even more prevalent among family members who take each other for granted, or are otherwise preoccupied, or are just too selfish to LISTEN.

These hurts: rejection from individuals, rejection from institutions, rejection from others not listening or not listening ourselves, are the result of a lack of love or compassion for our fellowman. Jesus put it this way:

> *As the Father hath loved me, so have I loved you: continue ye in my love. If ye keep my commandments, ye shall abide in my love; even as I have kept my Father's commandments, and abide in his love. These things have I spoken unto you, that my joy might remain in you, and that your joy might be full. This is my commandment, That ye love one another, as I have loved you. Greater love hath no man than this, that a man lay down his life for his friends. Ye are my friends, if ye do whatsoever I command you.* (**John 15:9-14**)

The phrase, *"lays down his life for his friends,"* means that one is being unselfish in his relationships with others. He is thinking more about others than he is about getting his own way or making his own point. It means that we become "good" listeners and not only able to hear what others are saying, but also willing to do our best to understand their thoughts and point of view. What a difference this would make in "family" relationships alone, if husbands and wives, children and parents, would only make the effort to "hear" and understand what the other members of the family were feeling and thinking. That is another subject we deal with in other books that my husband and I have written.

CHAPTER THREE

CRITICISM

Bless Those Who Persecute You

Matthew 5:44 *But I say unto you, Love your enemies, bless them that curse you, do good to them that hate you, and pray for them which despitefully use you, and persecute you;* (Matthew 5:44)

This chapter discusses criticism (including its different forms), why it is given, and how we can manage its contents.

I suppose one of the main hurts that people receive is in the criticisms they get. Whether it be constructive, which consists of honesty, (the old saying "the truth hurts,") or whether it be sarcasm, which consists of debasement; IT STILL HURTS.

The Bible has a lot to say about criticism. It addresses constructive criticism and destructive criticism. Constructive criticism is found in the following verses:

He is in the way of life that keepeth instruction: but he that refuseth reproof erreth. (Proverbs 10:17).

HURTING AND HEALING

> *The ear that heareth the reproof of life abideth among the wise. He that refuseth instruction despiseth his own soul: but he that heareth reproof getteth understanding.* (Proverbs 15:31-32)

In other words, if you profit from constructive criticism you will be elected to the wise men's hall of fame. But to reject criticism is to harm yourself and your own best interests!

> *As an earring of gold, and an ornament of fine gold, so is a wise reprover upon an obedient ear.* (Proverbs 25:12)

In other words, don't refuse to accept criticism; get all the help you can. It is a badge of honor to accept valid criticism.

> *He, that being often reproved hardeneth his neck, shall suddenly be destroyed, and that without remedy.* (Proverbs 29:1)

In other words, the man who is often reproved but refuses to accept criticism will suddenly be broken and never have another chance.

When you are criticized for doing something and there is a ring of truth to it, all you need to do is to be honest with yourself. Simply say, "You're right! I need to work on that." Or, "I agree, I haven't been doing my best." When you agree, the one criticizing understands that you have heard what he or she was talking about and

CHAPTER 3: CRITICISM

will back off. However, if you become defensive and try to rationalize your situation, you not only make matters worse in the relationship, but you deny the truth.

A mother was relating a story to me the other day. She told me that she and her teenage daughter were driving down the road and the mother decided to take this quality time to instruct her daughter on how to handle her finances. Her daughter had just gotten a new job. The mother proceeded to tell the teenager what to do with her money, but in a very domineering way. When the mother finished, the daughter was angry and said some indignant words to her mother and finished with, "It's my money and I think I should spend it the way I want to!" The daughter had expressed this feeling earlier in the conversation, but the mother just kept on talking—ignoring the statement. When the daughter finished, the mother pulled the car to the side of the road and almost slapped her daughter for talking to her like that (but she remembered the braces), so she just jerked her, and shrieked, "Don't you ever talk to me like that!" When they got to their destination, the mother got out of the car and told the young lady to stay in the car and think about what they were talking about. She hoped the child would come to her way of thinking. About forty-five minutes later, when the mother returned to the car, she inquired, "Have you given some thought to the way you talked to your mother?" The daughter replied, "Yes, I have been thinking about it and I feel like you can't accept criticism." The mother thought for a minute and said, "Maybe you are right." "I was so intent on your understanding what I was saying, that I wasn't listening to what you were saying." By this time, they had both calmed down and the Mother quietly said that the reason she was telling her daughter those ideas was because she loved her and felt it was her responsibility to teach her how to handle her money. Then she said, "But it is your choice. You do with your money what you wish." Now the daughter was in the listening mode and said that she would try to handle her finances like her mother was instructing her. This illustrates the way constructive criticism works. How agreeing with the criticizer can change the atmosphere to one of receptivity and therefore, be resolved in an amicable way.

There are some people who enjoy making jest of others, or some are jealous of others and can't stand their success and happiness.

There is that speaketh like the piercings of a sword: but the tongue of the wise is health. (Proverbs 12:18)

Some people like to make cutting, damaging remarks, but the words of the wise soothe and heal.

Other people go the route of trying to get even. They retaliate. They want to return evil for evil. These are the ones who spend weary days and sleepless nights brooding over their resentments, trying to hatch ways of getting even.

CHAPTER 3: CRITICISM

There is the interesting story of the grizzly bear, so strong that it can whip any animal in the west...except the buffalo and the Kodiak bear. Only one animal will the grizzly bear allow to eat with it, the SKUNK! The skunk has brazen impudence, and someone observed that the bear did not try to get even with him for eating its food. The grizzly instinctively knew the "high cost" of getting even.[2]

If we could realize the "high cost" of getting even, how it affects our bodies, how it sabotages our relationships with family and friends. We would quickly learn a better way of managing our hurts.

Mr. Tate was a man who considered himself a fine Christian. He attended all the services of the church. He experienced a stroke which left him paralyzed in one leg and with a speech impairment. He learned, through the minister's message, that bitterness and resentments play a role in various diseases, such as strokes. He wanted the minister to know that he had no bitterness or resentment towards anyone. That was not why he suffered his stroke. And yet, as he talked with the minister, he did admit that well, yes, maybe he was a little bitter over the fact that the Lord had taken his dear wife the year before. By the time the two had finished talking, Mr. Tate had confessed to a considerable amount of bitterness and hate. After talking about it and being honest with himself, he called the minister a few days later and told him that he had never felt better and that his

---

[2] S.I. McMillen, M.D., <u>None Of These Diseases</u> (Old Tappan: Fleming H. Revell Company, 1979), p. 67.

depression and worry were gone. He had confessed to God what he was feeling and asked God to cleanse him and make him whole again, not necessarily in body, but in spirit.

As a minister's wife, and in the public domain I have been the recipient of numerous cutting remarks. Many of them were from people who were jealous of me (I would eventually discover) or did not like the security I had in God, myself, and in my marriage. Once, my husband Page was preaching a series of sermons on the subject of the home. We have found this to be a very touchy subject. He used some of the material from my published book, <u>HUSBANDS</u>. Later, a lady who was having serious problems in her own marriage, remarked to some of our elders before the next worship service, "Well, I wonder if the minister will be preaching from St. Paul or St. Patti this morning?" Ouch! that hurt! I did forgive her, but I must admit I quickly lost respect for her.

Many times when people are trying to be funny, they express piercing remarks. Most of the time, it is their anger and resentment erupting. I have been in groups before and in the midst of discussing the attributes of someone, a participant would comment, laughingly, "Oh, I just hate her!" In actuality the person was saying, "I hate myself for not being able to attain what the other person has achieved."

THE MORE SELFISH WE ARE, THE MORE HURTS WE WILL ENDURE! Selfish people are their own worst enemy. The more "rights" one lays claim

CHAPTER 3: CRITICISM

to, the more often one gets clobbered! By using the word "rights" I mean the idea of having one's own way, or thinking one's way is the <u>only</u> way.

When others make cutting remarks to us or about us, we simply need to remember that it is just their opinion, and not necessarily a fact or a truth. We may not respect the person making a caustic comment about us. It is a good idea to bring it before the Lord to check our motives and actions in the light of His love and truth.

Hurt is one way God has of helping us to grow and change. I discovered from various sources that there are basically three main reasons why people change:

(1) Because they are bored to death, or

(2) They are motivated by love, or

(3) They are hurting very deeply.

Unfortunately, most of us fit into the third category. But even in this category, we find that "hurting" can be a positive element in our lives. Even our physical pain helps us locate a trouble spot in our bodies which needs healing.

There are times when we are making statements, expressing our views or feelings or thoughts, that we inadvertently "hurt" another's feelings. One example of this happened in a Sunday school class when the teacher was dealing with the Biblical idea of divorce. The teacher was

HURTING AND HEALING

unaware of several couples in the class who were divorced, and some remarried. Some of them got hurt. It would have been better for them had they chosen not to get hurt or be hurt.

There are times when we do well to choose not to be hurt! I remember when we were residing in a small town in Georgia. We had invited the new Chamber of Commerce Executive Director and wife for dinner. They were a handsome young couple whom we enjoyed getting to know—learning about their experiences in life. The subject somehow got into politics. At the time we were Democrats. Our guests were Republicans and started really putting down the Democratic Party. We listened and appreciated hearing their comments and their thinking.

Following dinner, we went into the room we called our den, and sat by the fireplace and watched the fire burn as we talked. His wife wanted to view the rest of the house. It was a beautiful home that the church provides its ministers, called a manse. As we were all walking down the hall, they noticed our "brag wall."

This wall was decorated with pictures and honors that our family had achieved: pictures of our daughter in her majorette uniform and our son in his band uniform; framed certificates of our son being listed in <u>Who's Who in High Schools</u> and Page's listed in <u>Who's Who in Religion</u>, etc. As the young couple continued looking over our collection, the young man's face got red and he commenced to apologize. I then realized that he was standing

CHAPTER 3: CRITICISM

in front of the framed invitation of Jimmy Carter's Governor's Inaugural Ball and the large 11 X 14 certificate naming me Lieutenant Colonel, Aide De Camp, Governor's Staff, one of the ways he had of showing his appreciation to all who had worked for him during his campaign. John just stood there and keep on apologizing for what he had said earlier about the Democrats and hoped he had not hurt our feelings. I assured him that he had not, because we chose not to be hurt, and that I believe the old saying "to each his own."

He seemed relieved and we went on enjoying the evening together. Just because people have different political views does not mean that they cannot enjoy each other's company. This does show that when we do not know one another, we sometimes say things about their relatives, friends, or maybe even their convictions, that could cause them hurt. In cases like this, it is good to choose not to have hurt feelings, so that the relationship is not damaged.

These can be growing experiences!

"And not only so, but we glory in tribulations also: knowing that tribulation worketh patience; And patience, experience; and experience, hope: And hope maketh not ashamed; because the love of God is shed abroad in our hearts by the Holy Ghost which is given unto us." (Romans 5:3-5)

HURTING AND HEALING

In other words, 'We can rejoice; too, when we run into problems, situations, and trials for we know that they are good for us. They help us learn to be patient and grow spiritually. And patience in circumstances develops strength of character in us and helps us trust God more each time we use it until finally our hope, faith, patience in circumstances and longsuffering with others are strong and steady. Then, when that happens, we are able to hold our heads high no matter what happens and know that all is well, for we know how dearly God loves us, and we feel this warm love everywhere within us because God has given us the Holy Spirit to fill our hearts with his love.'

Another form of criticism that is painful is in hearing what someone else said "about" you. Just know that when someone comes to you and begins rattling off what someone else said concerning you, that they probably feel the same way; therefore, they are actually telling you this information because they can blame someone else with it. Not only do they manage to tell you what was said, but they embellish it too. One of the key questions I usually ask someone when they start telling me something someone else said about me is this, "Do you believe that too?" It really takes them back and puts them into shock.

I had a lady call me one evening crying and almost hysterical. She explained that she was in a club and she couldn't go to a particular meeting. The next day three people had called her and informed her that the whole time was spent talking

CHAPTER 3: CRITICISM

about her. They went so far as to tell her the things that were said. I prayed a silent prayer to be able to know how to counsel her, but also for the tremendous hurt I knew she was feeling. I explained to her that she would have to forgive all of the ladies and pray and let God know she was hurt and that she needed to pray for them, as well. I quoted the Scripture, "If someone mistreats you because you are a Christian, don't curse him; pray that God will bless him: (Romans 12:14 TLB). I also felt like some of the accusations were so far out of line that she should call some of the ladies and confront them. She said she would pray about it. Several weeks later, when I saw her in the grocery store she said she prayed about the situation and asked God to bless them and then she called everyone that was at the meeting and confronted them. Some of them denied saying anything, some asked for forgiveness and some were rude to her because she called them on the "carpet," so to speak. But she herself felt much better.

I think it is so important that when you are hurt by someone who has mistreated you, that you tell the person, "OUCH, that hurts my heart." Maybe they meant to hurt you and if they did they will say so, if they didn't they will ask for forgiveness. It is so important not to let hurts pile up for then they become bitterness and resentment.

Follow peace with all men, and holiness, without which no man shall see the Lord: Looking diligently lest any man fail of the grace of God; lest any root of bitterness springing up trouble you, and thereby many be defiled; (Hebrews 12:14-15)

It is so easy to go into self-pity when you are hurt. Jesus taught:

> *Blessed are ye, when men shall revile you, and persecute you, and shall say all manner of evil against you falsely, for my sake. Rejoice, and be exceeding glad: for great is your reward in heaven: for so persecuted they the prophets which were before you.* (Matthew 5:11-12)

This is the reason it is good to confess to God about your hurt feelings. Some people say, "Well, it's not the criticism so much as the way people say it." This is a truth. I was in the grocery store one day when I was spoken to very harshly by some stranger. I was standing in front of the section of salad dressing and in trying to cut down on the grocery bill, was comparing prices, when I took one brand off the shelf and started to unscrew the top and smell it. I had planned on buying it, but just wanted to make sure it was what I wanted. I was no sooner getting ready to lift the top off when an elderly man very harshly yelled out, "You can't take the top off that, it's against the law!" I felt like he continued to growl at me. Well, everyone on the aisle looked at me. I quickly put the jar in my grocery cart and thanked the man for his information. I was so humiliated. It took several aisles of praying before I could forgive him. I wished he would have just nudged me and winked at me and said, "Hey, don't take the tops off—it's against

CHAPTER 3: CRITICISM

the law." I really felt badly that he let three aisles know about it. I agree with the information, it was just his way of presenting it that was so painful.

Have you ever been hurt, but you had asked for it? I have a friend who works for a community leader. This leader was coming under attack from business and towns people alike for a certain stand he was taking in his politics. My friend joked with him about it one afternoon and he turned on her like a devil's advocate. Her remark was in total innocence—yet he took it the wrong way. He took his wrath out on her. What she said didn't warrant such a lashing. Needless to say, she was hurt to the core. As we talked about it several days later, I asked her if she could forgive him. She said yes because later she learned what a terrible strain he had been under, yet she was having a hard time forgiving herself. She knew better than to tease and she usually wasn't the type to tease anyone and she was more angry with herself. If she had never teased him she wouldn't have this terrible hurt and possible broken relationship. Sometimes people use teasing in innocence or even in a form of anger and the result is painful.

Criticism can be POSITIVE. I learned early in our ministry that as a minister's wife I was certainly open for all kinds of criticism. Many an afternoon I would lie across the bed and cry and work myself into a sick headache as a result of what someone did or said to me. Thank God I am growing. I have now learned when I am criticized to evaluate it, and if it is valid, then *try* to change and if it is not valid, to forget it. Maturity is growing and if we don't learn to change we become inflexible and stagnate. This does not mean we are to be wishy-washy. But rather to allow room for growth in all areas of our life.

We have friends who are in a business together. The two men had some conflict and one of the men criticized the other man for losing customers. It was a legitimate criticism. The way the man was treating the customers was way out of line. Now, because one could not receive constructive criticism, he became a handicap for the associate by ignoring him completely. Can you imagine a business operating on that basis? Their secretary made the remark, "It is hard working in a business where the men are so childish!" She can see the humor in their childishness. But how pitiful it is. One is hurt by criticism and the other is hurt by being ignored. Where will it stop? The business suffers and the customers suffer.

The next time you are put into a situation and hurt by criticism, let the old spirit of getting even be replaced by the Holy Spirit of Christ, who when He was reviled, reviled not again. The Bible puts it this way:

> *For even hereunto were ye called: because Christ also suffered for us, leaving us an example, that ye should follow his steps: Who did no sin, neither was guile found in his mouth:* **Who, when he was reviled, reviled not again; when he suffered, he threatened not; but committed himself to him that**

CHAPTER 3: CRITICISM

__judgeth righteously:__ Who his own self bare our sins in his own body on the tree, that we, being dead to sins, should live unto righteousness: by whose stripes ye were healed. For ye were as sheep going astray; but are now returned unto the Shepherd and Bishop of your souls. (1 Peter 2:21-25)

A critical person is usually the one who is unconsciously most critical of himself. He doesn't like himself and when he gets upset with his own self-hate, he projects the rest onto those about him in the form of criticism. How critical are you?

One thing about criticism - expect it. There is no way to please everyone. Our main function in life is to please our Heavenly Father. If we are pleasing him, the opinions of others will not matter that much.

I think a beautiful illustration about worrying about the criticism of others was during the time when the Apostle Paul founded the thriving Church at Corinth. After he moved on, a brilliant orator, Apollos, became the pastor. The members compared Paul to this excellent preacher, and remarked:

For his letters, say they, are weighty and powerful; but his bodily presence is weak, and his speech contemptible. (2 Corinthians 10:10)

Paul's response to the Corinthian Church:

But though I be rude in speech, yet not

HURTING AND HEALING

in knowledge; but we have been throughly made manifest among you in all things. (2 Corinthians 11:6)

There is the old saying "to escape criticism - say nothing, do nothing, be nothing." At that point we would have to be "dead." But we are very much "alive" and want to continue growing and changing into what GOD'S WILL IS FOR US. I agree with Carra Harris,

"let's let God be our PUBLIC OPINION!"[3]

---

[3] S. I. McMillen, M.D., <u>None Of These Diseases</u> (Old Tappan: Fleming H. Revell Company, 1979), p.67.

CHAPTER FOUR

ROOTS

Lest Any Root of Bitterness Springing Up Trouble You (Hebrews 12:15)

This chapter reflects upon our upbringing and background and how it plays an intricate role in our relationships and self-confidence.

Anita sat on the sofa sobbing bitterly as I tried to console her. She was now twenty years old and had been an alcoholic since she was fifteen. She had tried just about everything and still felt lost and hopeless. She had only been a Christian a little over a year and had been able to cope with alcohol by being on a medicine, Antabuse. Then the power of the Holy Spirit gave her self-discipline. Her problem now was applying the Christian principles in her life. She was having a difficult time forgiving her parents. They were both alcoholics in their early fifties and died within a year of each other. They seldom showed Anita love and had not given her much loving discipline. It seemed like all her behavior patterns were negative. It was easy to BLAME her parents. She was hurt by the lack of parental love and attention she felt she needed. Even more so now after their deaths, she really felt abandoned! At this particular time in her life she was having difficulty with her job. She was having a hard time coming under authority. Not having had any authoritative discipline, now at the age of twenty, learning to come under authority was really getting her down.

I said, "Anita, you're going to have to confess your hurt to God and forgive your parents." She said, "How can I? In everything I've ever done or tried to do they rejected me. They said I was the cause of all their problems. They were so selfish," she sobbed. I responded, "I realize that, but you have to forgive them so God can forgive you. You cannot go on BLAMING your parents for the difficulty you are having now. You have to be responsible for yourself," I insisted.

"I never thought about having to be responsible for myself," she replied. I exclaimed, "Yes, you did come up through childhood with feelings of being unloved and with some negative behavior patterns. However, you are accountable for your own sins. You can change those into positive behavior patterns and be a different person. You don't have to be the person you think they made of you. Be the person God wants you to be. Seek His guidance and ask His Holy Spirit to change you and to help you come under His authority, and also the authority of those in your workplace. He helped you with doing away with alcohol, I know He can help you understand authority." We are, all of us, the product of those parents who loved us or failed or refused to love us. Many times, when we come from BACKGROUNDS of unloving parents, we have a hard time learning to come under authority. We have a

CHAPTER 4: ROOTS

difficult time becoming involved, because we don't want to be HURT anymore. We don't want to assume responsibility because assuming responsibility means getting criticized. Who needs that HURT. It is difficult to talk about unloving parents, but we have to face reality. If the parents do not love the Lord, they don't understand what love IS. They are incapable of real love, because GOD IS LOVE. It isn't that they mean to be selfish, but they don't know any other way. People who come up in a family with little love are very sensitive people. They are super-sensitive, and therefore, their HURTS are deeper and more frequent. These people, when they are HURT, need to tell God they are hurt and He will reveal to them that they need to ask God's forgiveness, and forgive those who hurt them.

Our family likes to go camping. One year when we were camping in Montreal, Canada, in one of their beautiful parks, we met a couple camping right next to us. We drank coffee around the campfire and talked about things in general. One night, Andrew started talking about his background. His father died when Andrew was fifteen years old. It left him to help care for his mother. Because of having to go to school and work, he did not get all the counsel and guidance that many young men get in preparation for graduation or college. So, he joined the armed service and stayed in the service two years before coming home with a medical discharge. He started to work at the local paper mill. He is in his early forties and still working at the paper mill. He is resentful and bitter about it. He did

HURTING AND HEALING

not like his job. More than that he didn't like himself, because he feels he isn't worth much in society. He is bitter because someone did not take the time to counsel him during his teen years. We talked at some length with him, mainly asking questions. When we finally came to the end of our conversation, and Andrew was about talked out, he said, "I guess all these years I've been blaming someone else for what I'm doing today. I never realized it until now, but I could have changed the course of my vocation any time I wanted to. You know, when I get back to my home, I'm going to do some investigating into different jobs and vocations.

Months later, we got a letter from Kansas. We were wondering who we knew in Kansas. It was form Andrew. He had gone home and started looking and praying about going into another job. Eventually, he went into the insurance business and was so good at selling it, that he got his own company and was now happy as could be. He was grateful to us for listening to him and the fact that he was able to go back into his childhood to discover why he felt as he did.

We need to realize that many people use their BACKGROUND to nurture their hurt. So many people say, "That's the way I am, you knew that when you married me." In a marriage or other relationships when people feel this way, there is not much hope. Growing is changing and maturing, but if people hold on to their backgrounds, there is little room for change. God wants us to be able to change.

CHAPTER 4: ROOTS

It is written in Ephesians,

> *And be renewed in the spirit of your mind; And that ye put on the new man, which after God is created in righteousness and true holiness. (Ephesians 4:23-24)*

So, don't blame your background for the hurts you are suffering. According to God's word, we can change if we decide to do so.

I know how difficult it makes it for a person to feel he is unwanted at home. Many times, I hear a mother express, "I don't need another mouth to feed in this house." A mother or father who expresses that in front of the child does not realize what this message gives to the child. It is like planting a seed of insecurity in that child's heart.

One teenager told us that his mother was pregnant again for the seventh time, and she cried and kept saying she didn't want the baby. How hard it was for him to understand, because he got the feeling that she probably felt the same thing about him when he was conceived. It created within him the uneasy feeling of not being wanted or loved.

We knew of one young man who overheard his parents fighting one night. "You didn't have to marry me just because I was pregnant," yelled the mother. "Yes, I did! Your parents would have me put in jail if I hadn't married you," the father shouted back. Enough was enough. Dink had heard his parents fight many times. This was the first time he heard them make such statements. It hurt his heart to the core to think that he was unwanted and a mistake. To think that he may have been conceived out of selfishness and lust. He began to brood about it. He lost weight. His grades dropped in school. Finally, he couldn't handle the facts any longer and started on drugs. He wanted to punish his parents—and punish them he did. He got into all kinds of trouble and finally used his dad's shotgun to kill himself. A young person's bad behavior and ugly attitudes may have more to do with his background that we ordinarily suspect.

In like manner, a person's poor health and general outlook on life could be conditioned by his background. I talked recently with a man sixty-five years old who was having severe health problems. He was having bladder problems, arthritis in his hands and legs, weight problems, but most of all, he was angry and bitter. He had not seen his mother in seven years although he lived in the same town. His mother was in a nursing home and she was asking to see him. He really didn't want to see her. When I asked him why, he related the following story. "When I was ten years old, my parents divorced. My mother left my sister and me with my grandmother. My mother moved fifteen hundred miles away. She only saw me on holidays and did not write. She missed all my school plays and honors that I received in my higher level of school. My grandmother raised me and my sister, and when she died, I felt all alone. As I grew older, my wife and I tried to establish a relationship with my mother, which we did, but mostly because of the closeness I had with my step-father. However, my

CHAPTER 4: ROOTS

step-father was accidently killed at the age of only thirty-eight. Once again, I felt I had no family because the link between me and my mother was now gone. I had two children of my own, but I found myself acting cold and callous even toward them, just as my mother had acted toward me."

Here was this sixty-five year old man now with his own married children, having moved away, and yet, longing for a family just as he had longed for a family years before. As we talked, he poured out his heart (confession is good for the soul) and in so doing, he realized that he had been blaming his own mother for his feelings of unhappiness for all these years. We prayed together. He told God that he was forgiving his mother for leaving him as a child. Weeping as he prayed, he asked God to forgive him for remaining so long in his childish role, and for his anger and bitterness toward his mother. He was now doing as the Apostle Paul said that he did,

> *When I was a child, I spake as a child, I understood as a child, I thought as a child: but when I became a man, I put away childish things.* (1 Corinthians 13:11)

Several weeks later, I met this same man in one of our shopping centers—I hardly recognized him. His whole countenance had changed from a drawn frown to a bright smile. Even his stride was much faster. I remarked to him how well he looked. He was so excited and apologized for not calling and letting me know what had happened. He told me that he had gone to see his mother in the nursing home. "The visit was so wonderful," he exclaimed. He let me know about his plans to work very hard at establishing a good relationship with his mother and how grateful he was that his mom still had such a good mind so that they could talk and enjoy being together. These are the kind of experiences I take delight in hearing about, and hopefully, anyone reading about this story will be able to find relief from their background as well.

There is another kind of hurt, which I think is one of the most painful that a person has to endure—it is the hurt that comes from rebellion. Rebellion is so prevalent in today's society; it seems that almost everyone is rebelling against something or someone. Most of my discussion on this subject of hurt by ROOTS and BACKGROUND has dealt with how children are affected. But now, I would like to show some blood, sweat, and tears that some parents have had over their rebellious children. God makes it known to us just how serious rebellion is when we read,

> *For rebellion is as the sin of witchcraft, and stubbornness is as iniquity and idolatry. Because thou hast rejected the word of the LORD, he hath also rejected thee from being king.* (1 Samuel 15:23)

The parents I am talking about are Christians; they have sought to bring their children up in the nurture and admonition of the Lord. Yet as their children grow into their teens, they become bombarded with television, news media, and peer pressure. So many teenagers become the recipients

CHAPTER 4: ROOTS

of rebellion.

I sat trying to console a sobbing mother, and I felt the pain and hurt as she began telling her story. They were what we would call "middle class" people. They were family oriented. They went to church and they participated in their children's activities. They encouraged family counsels and family outings. They were open and honest with their teenagers and expected it in return. However, at the age of ten, Joanne had already begun to rebel. She was very young to be so stubborn, so the whole family immediately went for family counseling. Things settled down for a while, but then at the age of fifteen, Joanne began staying out all night. Then she began staying away from home two and three days at the time. She had a "so-called" boyfriend, and ended up sleeping with him in a tent for eight weeks in a deserted campground. The parents went everywhere for help, trying everything. Joanne finally got tired and came back home. As glad as the parents were, the child continued to disrupt the family. She drank a lot of beer, smoked pot and got mixed up with another boy who was much older. She landed in court several times and was finally put in a youth hall (detention home). She spent two months in the youth hall, and hoping she had been rehabilitated, Joanne returned to her family. They put her in a private school and did everything they could for her. She finally skipped so much school that she didn't graduate. She eventually got her high school diploma from the community college GED program. She

HURTING AND HEALING

continued to cause the parents trouble, to the point that they had different opinions on how Joanne should be handled. Here she is now, eighteen, with no job, no goals, no morals and yet, her behavior continues to hurt her parents.

The hurt, the pain, the anger goes so deep, time after time. What can a parent do?

Our children are an extension of us. When they fail, it hurts us as well as them. Teens today feel like they must try everything for themselves. No matter how you teach them values and morals—some tend to rebel and do their own thing. They have no idea that this rebellion against authority is a sin against God.

On another occasion, a fifteen-year-old girl was sitting in my office, her head bowed low. She mumbled answers to the questions I was asking of her. She was pregnant, said she loved the boy – yet, he didn't want to marry her. Even though she was a Christian, she didn't feel she sinned. She thought, because she "loved" the boy, that it was O.K. She knew better, but all her friends were doing it, and now, she was caught. That was the only remorse she felt. Not that she sinned, but that she was caught.

Roots, background, upbringing, home—all of these play an important part in a person's makeup. The many hurts we face today are the result of our past. But thank God we can do as the Apostle Paul did.

CHAPTER 4: ROOTS

> *Brethren, I count not myself to have apprehended: but this one thing I do, <u>forgetting those things which are behind, and reaching forth unto those things which are before, I press toward the mark for the prize of the high calling of God in Christ Jesus</u>.* (Philippians 3:13-14)

We need to put our background in the past and draw some insights from it, but never blame it on anyone for our position in life. We need to be mature and responsible for who we are and what we are in society today. It is not the problem in our lives that is important, but how we handle the problem that counts the most.

It seems like parents go from the extreme of being too strict, to being too uncaring. Those who were brought up in a home where the parents didn't care what they did or who they did it with or when they did it, are people who have a fixation on being children forever and always are dependent on others. They may become dependent on alcohol, drugs, or anything to help them escape. But they mostly become dependent on others. They go from group to group, person the person, acting the part of the dependent child, wanting people to tell them what to do. Then rebelling against it. These people become like a leech. They smother friendships or relationships because they are so dependent. They want others to make decisions for them.

Alan is a case in point. He was the last of eight children in the home. By the time he came along his parents were getting on in age and just let Alan make his own way in the household. They never seemed to care where he was or with whom. They hardly ever disciplined him; they didn't seem to encourage him or affirm him in any way. So never having gone through being a "child" in the sense of parental discipline and love, Alan became fixed in the child role. As he grew into adulthood, he smothered his wife by wanting her to mother him, telling him the do's and don'ts of life. They had two children and it was impossible for her to care for the children and Alan in the way he wanted her to. So Alan started going to counselors and group sessions, from one to another. It wasn't until he realized he was still living in the child role that he began to change. It was only he who could change. The counselors couldn't do it for him. But before he did change, he went through quite a mental and emotional strain depending on others to "parent" him. It wasn't until he realized, through Christ's help, that he could change. He eventually became the man God wanted him to be. He learned to depend on God for his decisions, for his acts, his thoughts and his divine discipline. Alan admitted that he felt comfortable, yet miserable in the child role. It was a "comfort zone" for him. He kept thinking that change meant hurt. He was hurt that his parents didn't give him the guidance he needed to make him grow up and mature. He resented the fact that they weren't Christians and that they had not taught him to depend on God. After Alan started maturing in his "faith" he went back to his parents and forgave them and taught them how to depend on Christ. He explained that

CHAPTER 4: ROOTS

someday when they are really old that they may want to depend on Alan, and he didn't want to be smothered. He wanted them to learn, at this point in their lives, to depend on Christ. He alone supplies all our needs.

HURTS OF THE PAST (family background) **NEED TO BE FORGIVEN AND FORGOTIEN AND USED TO GOD'S GLORY IN OUR LIVES**.

There are hurts in life that come when our parent dies. The child may feel cheated in life. Take the case of Becky. Both of her parents died by the time she was twenty years old. This young woman did not have an immediate family. She still needed guidance and love from a family relationship. Where would she spend her holidays? It seemed that everyone had someone but her. She felt left out at family night suppers at the church, she felt left out on holidays, she simply felt left out. How did she handle this? She began exercising her Christian "faith" in God and seeing Him as her Father who knows all things. She not only saw Him as her Savior, but her Father whom she looked to for guidance and warmth. As she began turning to Him, she began inviting people to her apartment. She looked for lonely people on holidays. She found an elderly couple that had never had children and she began giving them her attention and time. They responded to her warmth, so much so that they felt like family to her. On and on Becky gave of herself in helping others to overcome this feeling of loneliness. She mixed widows, divorcees, orphans and those who had

HURTING AND HEALING

families but who felt rejection. She has no organization going, but she has a lot of love and warmth and friends she might never have had if she had not reached out in the warmth she felt from her Heavenly Father. Until she marries and has her own family, she has the family of God that she is creating, and many people are being touched by her life.

Becky learned how to overcome the hurt of not having an immediate family and has grown further into the tree of life.

CHAPTER FIVE

SEPARATION

And he said unto me, My grace is sufficient for thee: for my strength is made perfect in weakness. Most gladly therefore will I rather glory in my infirmities, that the power of Christ may rest upon me. (2 Corinthians 12:9)

This chapter involves an in-depth look with regard to separation; it may be attributed to death, divorce, or emotional duress. After our hearts have been filled with pain following separation, the initial healing process begins with the attainment of a humble spirit as we come before God.

"The shrill of the telephone ringing in the middle of the night caused me and Al to sit straight up in the bed, cringing and fumbling for the phone," Betty said, as she related to me a horrifying experience that had happened to her a few years earlier.

"Hello," Al answered, trying to get his bearings. "Yes, this is Al Beech. Just a minute, let me write that down."

I saw the puzzled look on Al's face and watched as he hung up the phone. "Well, who was it?" I asked.

HURTING AND HEALING

"I'm not sure. I thought they said it was the coroner's office, but I'm sure that's not what they said. Anyway, they told me to call this number in New York."

"Whose number is it?" I inquired, half asleep and stunned from the sound of the ringing phone.

Al started dialing the number, and I dozed off because he had to wait and dial again because it was busy. Al forgot about the time difference between California and New York. But finally someone answered.

"Hello, this is Al Beech in California, and I was asked to call this number. What did you say? I'm sorry, there must be some mistake. It's impossible - you're sure - call back later?"

Al turned white and looked at me, "It's the coroner's office in New York, and they say our daughter's body is in their morgue. I'm sure they are mistaken, but I couldn't get any more information, and they told me to call back later."

Our stomachs were churning, but the coffee helped as we sat talking and watching the clock tick away the minutes that seemed like hours. It just couldn't be our Darlene that they were talking about—surely it was a case of mistaken identity. Darlene was such a sweet gal. Very quiet and seemed to love life. She was now working in New York, that is true, but we had just talked with her several days ago, and everything was going so well with her. She was thinking about flying out to

CHAPTER 5: SEPARATION

California to visit with us as soon as her next assignment was over. She was employed with a magazine company, had a lot of talent, and a good future with the company.

Finally, at eight a.m. New York time, we could not stand it any longer, so Al started dialing the number again.

"Yes, this is Al Beech, I'm calling about a report of my daughter - I just know there must be some mistake you have; well let me talk to him."

Al talked with the police officer who said he had found Darlene's body in her apartment and that she had taken an overdose of pills. He said that her apartment was on his beat and that one of the neighbors had asked him to go up and check on her because they had not seen her in several days.

What a shock! You can't imagine as a mother or father, the pain and hurt we felt. We actually could not believe it until we saw her in the casket. My heart ached so badly and I felt so burdened that I did not know if I could make it through the funeral services or not.

After the funeral some of the shock was gone, yet there lingered the questioning hurt of WHY? Why did this happen? Where did we as parents go wrong? What did we do?

Even now, after two years, I still feel the ache and pain and hurt. If she was unhappy, then why did she not discuss this with us? My husband believed that if she would have just discussed her feelings with us that he could have talked her out of doing such a thing. All the thoughts go through our minds even now. Our darling, Darlene, had put some money in a savings account and told us that she wanted to buy some property near our home someday. Now, ironically, that money went to buy a cemetery plot not far from our home.

The above story illustrates one of the strongest hurts of all—that of SEPARATION. This sweet couple was deeply hurt and felt the terrible pain of separation as a result of their daughter's death. Death is a final separation on earth and a most difficult one to handle. So, let's talk about how to handle this kind of HURT.

First of all, there is the need for us to simply admit to God that we hurt and that the pain is unbearable. We must admit to it, experience it, feel it, and then ask and THANK God for making us strong enough to be able to endure it.

When separation by death occurs, we tend to go through certain stages. We usually go through denial, then through self-pity, then through some anger and finally come to the point of acceptance. We go through all kinds of feelings, such as: shock, grief, regret, sorrow, worry, fear, anger, bitterness, and resentment. If these feelings are left to harbor in our hearts, they cause our souls to go sour and we miss out on the real meaning and purpose of life, which is to Glorify God and enjoy Him forever. My suggestion to you is to simply bundle all these

CHAPTER 5: SEPARATION

mixed bag of feelings up and hand them over to your Heavenly Father, who will take them from us, and, miracle of miracles, transform them into a healing of your soul, and even into joy and thanksgiving.

After a safe period of time, some shorter than for others, but not over too long a period of time, begin to "think" about other things. Every time you think of your loved one, shoot up a prayer and say something like this: "Dear Father, I cannot think about her (him) right now and I thank you for helping me think about something else." In asking Him to help you change your thought patterns, you may find yourself doing this hundreds of times a day. Finally, God will take away the thoughts that ultimately leads to the terrible PAIN AND HURT. It is good to have grief and it is okay to reflect back and even okay to ask why, but do not linger in that mode for too long. Move on and live in the moment, each day.

There are many forms of SEPARATION, death is not the only one. A letter came to me not long ago from a woman who lives in Australia. She had read my book, <u>HUSBANDS</u>, and she wanted me to hear her story and see if I had any advice I could give her in her particular situation. She related to me that her husband had been fired from his job and subsequently disappeared. It was now eight months later. She did not know whether he was dead or alive. She had a lot of good things to say about him; she declared that she loved him and would take him back, even if he had left her for another woman. She had gone through eight months of severe pain from this mysterious separation. Not only did the wife go through much suffering, but her pain was compounded because of her children. Their father was absent; one who had brought them into the world was now gone. They had been abandoned—what humiliation. As I read this ladies letter, my heart went out to her. There were many unanswered questions which she asked me. Why did he do it? Why was he fired? What was he afraid of? Does he not love me or his children anymore? Is he mentally sick? Where is he? What do we do, and how can we cope?

Separation is hard to cope with. But it seems that it could be that that couple had already been separated, emotionally and spiritually, for quite some time—even before this man took off. There must have been something in their marriage about which they could not communicate. Maybe he was under guilt, thus causing him a mental and emotional strain which led to the separation. Whatever the cause, the thing now was to teach the wife how to handle the separation. In Dr. Larry Crabbs book, <u>BASIC PRINCIPLES ON BIBLICAL COUNSELING,</u> he stresses that it is not the problem in our life, but how we handle the problem that counts.

It is so hard to understand God's plan of the universe and to understand that the solution to all problems is a "spiritual" solution. Too often, we human beings are born, marry, and get old, without ever giving thought to the "plan of God"

CHAPTER 5: SEPARATION

and His involvement in our lives or in this world. We must always go to the Scriptures to discover the purpose of pain and suffering.

It helps us in our daily lives if we truly believe what Paul writes:

> "And we know that all things work together for good to them that love God, to them who are the called according to His purpose" (Romans 8:28).

God's purpose for our being here is for us to "enjoy Him and for Him to enjoy us", both now and forever. The question is, how can He enjoy us if we don't acknowledge Him, if we don't even know He is around? He enjoys us when we take the time to communicate with Him during the days of our lives. When we go through life ignoring Him, then He has to allow certain hurts, pain, tragedies, and so on, to happen to us so that He can get our attention. There are some people who never give God their attention and, of course, they are eternally separated from Him, which is a living Hell.

Many of our pains and hurts are brought on ourselves, because we don't live by the Divine principles set forth in His Word. However, He allows the innocent as well as the unjust to experience pain for the purpose of being reconciled with Him. When the bumps of life come, we can become "bitter" or "better"! We can have pain and become "blessed" or "burned" through the experience. To become blessed we must say with Job,

HURTING AND HEALING

> *"Though he slay me, yet will I trust him: but I will maintain mine own ways before him"* (Job 13:15).

We continue to look to Him regardless of the circumstances or regardless how much pain we are experiencing, and even if we can't see "daylight" in the situation. We simply go on in "faith," believing and knowing that He is working it out for our good so that we will communicate with Him and He can enjoy us now and forever. He wants not only a foxhole kind of prayer and relationship, but one in which He can enjoy us on a constant basis.

> *Rejoice evermore. Pray without ceasing. In every thing give thanks: for this is the will of God in Christ Jesus concerning you.* (1 Thessalonians 5:16-18)

I wrote back to the lady in Australia, explaining God's will for her being, and instructing her to devote her time to Christ, so that He can give her His Holy Spirit.

> *If ye love me, keep my commandments. And I will pray the Father, and he shall give you another Comforter, that he may abide with you for ever; Even the Spirit of truth; whom the world cannot receive, because it seeth him not, neither knoweth him: but ye know him; for he dwelleth with you, and shall be in you. I will not leave you comfortless: I will come to you. Yet a little while, and the world seeth me no more; but ye see me: because I live, ye shall live also. At that day ye shall know that I am in my Father, and ye in me, and I in you.* (John 14:15-20)

CHAPTER 5: SEPARATION

I indicated to her that the Holy Spirit will give her power and comfort to deal with the ordeal. She should realize that it is only through His power that she would be able to handle this hurt by separation. I expressed to her that she would do well to absorb her whole being in Christ and become dependent on Him. Too often, we make ourselves vulnerable to "hurt" by idolizing our spouse, and this displeases God because in His Word we are instructed that we are not to have any other gods before Him. When we are hurting severely enough, we will then be willing to put away the idols and seek His presence. We will then have the peace that passes all understanding, meaning that we may not always know "why" things happen the way they do, but we will know through this happening that we have come into a closer relationship with our Lord Jesus Christ and this is His plan for our lives. We must become broken in order to give up our self-will and come under God's authority. Before God can help us in time of pain and hurt or crisis, He must bring us to complete brokenness so that we will depend completely on Him. Until we are broken, we are so full of self that there is no room for God. Only God knows what experience it will take to bring us to Him. This is why we can actually be joyous in our hurts, pains, and sorrows, because we know He loves us enough to bring us closer to Him and teach us how to love one another.

This seems to be what James was teaching when he writes,

> *My brethren, count it all joy when ye fall into divers temptations; Knowing this, that the*

> *trying of your faith worketh patience. But let patience have her perfect work, that ye may be perfect and entire, wanting nothing.* (James 1:2-4)

Parents discipline their child so that the child won't get hurt by society. They can learn to bend their child's will, without breaking the child's spirit. If a child is not disciplined by his parents, to the point of bending the child's will—then it will be necessary for the school administration or the police force or the military or some other institution in society to do the disciplining. Parents who love their child will want everyone else to love him as they do, therefore, they see the necessity for correcting their child's behavior and attitudes. Oddly enough, the child will love his parents and respect them more if they teach him how to come under authority. This is the way God deals with His children, He teaches us through loving discipline, so we will love and respect Him and live with Him eternally. The writer of Hebrews put it this way:

> *And ye have forgotten the exhortation which speaketh unto you as unto children, My son, despise not thou the chastening of the Lord, nor faint when thou art rebuked of him: For whom the Lord loveth he chasteneth, and scourgeth every son whom he receiveth.* (Hebrews 12:5-6)

I am thinking now of a couple that Page and I spent many hours counseling. We discovered that both of them were very self-centered and

CHAPTER 5: SEPARATION

stubborn. Their marriage was very stormy due to their selfishness. The constant turmoil in the home contributed much to the emotional problems of their children. They were Christians, both living in the Spirit, but certainly not walking in the Spirit. Their marriage was into its ninth year, the last three were held together with the help of our counseling. After we moved to another state, they stopped seeking counsel, stopped worshipping at the church and stopped working on the marriage. Needless to say, the marriage finally deteriorated to the point that the young wife filed for a divorce. Because she would not listen to any more counsel, not talk with God, she fell victim to her own design and desire. The divorce was a big mess. The court scene was horrible. She got what she wanted—a divorce, the four children and the house. However, three months after the divorce she was pleading with her former husband to come back to her. She had treated him dreadfully—embarrassing him in front of the church, the community, his boss, and friends. She now realized her mistake and wanted him back. In the meantime, he was dating a fine Christian woman and learning to put God first in his life. This young wife, because of her stubbornness, will have to become completely broken and suffer the consequences of failing to listen to God and come under His leadership. She will pay dearly for her selfishness. But if she will turn to God for His guidance for her life and change her heart, perhaps the young man will see her change, and for the sake of the children go back to her. But the question is, is she willing to come under God's rule for her life? She hasn't been able to up to this time, but conceivably when she is hurting harshly enough, she will surrender all to Him. That is my prayer.

Hurt and pain often come from separation in the child-parent relationship. A young girl runs away from home. The parents are frantic, wondering where she is, and with whom, and is she alright? They are also angry and frustrated as to why she ran away to begin with. How could she do this to them? Out of their agony of rejection they may discover their selfishness and the mistakes they were making of which they were not even aware. They may begin looking at their unhappy lives together and realize that they have not been living under God's plan for their marriage, that they have not been bringing up their children in the nurture and counsel of the Lord. But by repentance and self-repudiation they could grow in fellowship with Him and with one another, which would bring about healing and restoration in the family unit. The cost of learning to love may be high, but God gives the rewards and they are eternal.

Pain and hurt can also come from separation when couples do not have the same interests, such as mental and spiritual separation. Somehow as human beings we have not learned God's purpose for marriage. Most people think they will marry and live happily ever after. One of God's purposes for giving marriage is to teach us how to love one another, to reduce us down to brokenness in order to produce sacrificial love in our hearts. God at the center of our home will

CHAPTER 5: SEPARATION

make the home united. If you have five people in the family and they are all taught the spiritual truths of putting God first in their lives—then when you have a problem, as all five go into prayer, all five will agree on the solution, thus making this family unit one. Couples could save an awful lot of hurt and pain in marriage and in relationships by putting Christ at the center of their lives.

Mental separation is one hurt that is hard to get a handle on. Ruby was a beautiful woman. She was a fine Christian and really loved the Lord. However, she noticed Bart was always gone. They had been married for 32 years and had an easy go of their marriage from all financial aspects. However, lately she observed that Bart was never home, plus when they were out in company he kept giving her awful digs about her cooking, cleaning and so forth. She couldn't communicate with him and he always buried himself in TV or slept when he was at home. He had nothing to say to her. He continued to give her the money she always wanted to decorate the home or fix herself up, but with the children gone, she felt so alone. Finally one day she went down to her husband's office to see if he would take her to lunch.

When she walked in unexpectedly, there he was embracing another woman in a way that she knew instinctively that he was involved with this woman. Ruby burst out crying. She felt the pain, the hurt, the humiliation, and realized all this time, the past two years, this must have been going on. Bart was mentally and emotionally separated from her and emotionally caught up with another woman. The pain was unbearable, all she could do was stand there and cry, and the hymn came to her as she repeated over and over again to herself, "Lord lift me up and let me stand, a higher plane than I have found, Lord plant my feet on higher ground." Days later the pain and hurt and trauma still wouldn't go away. She confronted Bart and requested him to tell every detail of the affair. She asked him to call the other woman's husband and give in detail what had gone on. She counseled with Bart and my, how painful it was. She kept thinking of Job and repeating,

> *"though he slay me, yet will I trust in him:..."* (Job 13:15 KJV).

She prayed without ceasing. How should she handle this hurt, this pain, this humiliation? She kept asking God to direct their paths. In the process of her pain, Ruby went through a re-evaluation of her own life. She thought about how she talked to God, but maybe never really knew Him. She remembered that scripture where it says something like, "Not all who sound religious are really godly people. They may refer to me as 'Lord', but still won't get to heaven. For the decisive question is whether they obey my Father in heaven."

> *Not every one that saith unto me, Lord, Lord, shall enter into the kingdom of heaven; but he that doeth the will of my Father which is in heaven.* (Matthew 7:21)

CHAPTER 5: SEPARATION

Ruby began realizing that all this time she claimed the Christian faith, and yet she had been idolizing her husband and putting him before God in her life. She confessed this idolatry to God and asked for cleansing and for the love of the Holy Spirit in her heart. She made a decision to forgive Bart and help him all she could. She asked the Lord to lift her up and let his shield of faith support her so she could bear the burden of an unfaithful husband. Through Ruby's and God's love, Bart did change. It was a long, slow, painful process. But today they are radiant in their faith! Oh, yes, they do have scare tissue of the soul, because of the affair, but the glory of the Lord shines around them as they put Him first place in their life and home. Now, just because she didn't put God first in her life was no reason for Bart to commit adultery, but in and through this pain and suffering, two people have come to know Him in a more complete way. Also they have been a testimony for others who have watched this couple overcome the sin of adultery and idolatry and become a lighthouse for His Word.

Before I leave the subject of mental separation, I must inject a few paragraphs on the idea of fantasy as a form of mental separation. If one partner in a marriage is pre-occupied with self or living in a fantasy world, there is a strong possibility of mental cruelty occurring. I'm not talking about the good creative and positive dreams you have that include your spouse. I'm saying that when one partner intentionally leaves the other out of his/her thinking, then he/she becomes indifferent

HURTING AND HEALING

to the needs and desires of the other. When a spouse indulges in sexual fantasy, or any other type of fantasy for gratification over the importance of the partner, then that spouse is being purely selfish. The mind, as I see it, is similar to a computer—"garbage in, garbage out." The subconscious mind will eventually act out what is fed into the conscious mind. If a spouse is continually thinking (engaged in fantasy) about someone else, that spouse will eventually act out those sinful thoughts. What this does is cause not only mental separation, but emotional and physical separation as well. One becomes double-minded when one becomes pre-occupied with selfish desires, and in so doing, neglects one's spouse or friend or family. This manifests itself in one as a feeling of going "crazy." One becomes two people—a split personality.

"I think I'm going crazy," Charlene cried as she sat in my office pouring out her heart. "Tom and I just argue and fight about everything," she sobbed as she vented her feelings about her marriage.

As I listened to Charlene tell me about their problems, I sat prayerfully asking for God's wisdom in the matter. When she paused to blow her nose, I looked her right in the eye and asked, "Is there someone else?"

She looked shocked, and cried, "Yes, but not really! You see, there is this man I work with who is so good looking and so nice to me. I have been thinking about him for four months now, and I can't keep my mind off of him. I don't like myself

CHAPTER 5: SEPARATION

for it, I know it's wrong. I guess it is ruining my marriage, and it's making me sick. Please help me, I just don't know what to do!"

Admitting it was a sin and asking for God's forgiveness was the first step for Charlene. I then taught her to re-program her mind. Every time she thought of him, even though it felt good to her, she must pray and ask God to forgive her and give her the strength to overcome the fantasy. Because she was so desperate to save her marriage, (this being her second one) and herself, she agreed to the prayer principle and the power principle of the Scripture:

"I can do all things through Christ which strengtheneth me" (Philippians 4:13).

Fortunately, this story has a happy ending. I recently talked with Charlene and discovered that God had healed her mind of her former fantasy world, and she and her husband are getting along beautifully.

Pain can have a purifying power. The apostle Peter put God's words into writing,

"For he that has suffered in the flesh hath ceased from sin." (1 Peter 4:1)

Because Charlene yielded to Christ and asked for His help, her pain was used to purify her mind. Having been exposed, she'd realized her sin, became convicted about the seriousness of the fantasy, and decided to cease from doing it. In this way her mind became purified. I believe that even someone like an alcoholic can have their mind purified, if they turn to Christ. The key here is that one has to recognize suffering in the flesh. Usually, this comes about when one is exposed and has the experience of suffering in the flesh. Sins of the flesh such as adultery, fornication, excessive drinking, and abuse of any kind, are very difficult to cope with. It is only when these sins are exposed and the person comes to his senses, turns his life over to Christ, and asks for God's help, that God then purifies the heart so that the person will not want to enter into that sin ever again.

> *But all things that are reproved are made manifest by the light: for whatsoever doth make manifest is light.* (Ephesians 5:13)

With Jesus Christ in our hearts and our relationship to God and the Holy Spirit working in us we can handle pain and hurt with supernatural reactions. Look up the story in Luke that tells about James and John wanting Jesus to call down fire on the Samaritan village that rejected Jesus and his Apostles. Jesus rebuked them saying,

> *"You don't know what manner of spirit you are of."* (Luke 9:55)

If we can see pain and hurt as growing and changing, then we can thank God for it. While Nan sat in the doctor's office waiting for the doctor to come out with her latest blood report, she looked over at Tim and wondered what the future would hold. This was the second time this month that they

CHAPTER 5: SEPARATION

sat waiting eagerly for a report - praying all would be well. She had not been feeling well these past few months and she didn't seem to have any strength. All she wanted to do was lie around and sleep, and that was unlike the bubbly Nan who was always jumping around taking in every minute of life.

The doctor came out. "I'm afraid this one is positive too. You do have a rare blood disease. I have had a consultation with three other doctors and our findings are all the same and we are in agreement."

"Just what does all this mean?" Tim asked softly.

"It means that Nan has from one to maybe three years to live. There is nothing else we can do for her except make her as comfortable as possible.

Stunned and in a state of shock, Nan heard the voices, but couldn't believe they were discussing her life. She kept hearing the doctor's voice saying, "one to maybe three years to live," hoping she was just having a bad dream, and in a minute she would wake up and everything would be all right. But, facing stark reality, Nan knew it was her they were talking about.

Months later as Nan lay in bed wrestling with her medical problem, she had all kinds of thoughts go through her mind. As she wrestled with these thoughts, it reminded her of Jacob wrestling with the angel. Jacob wouldn't let go until the angel

HURTING AND HEALING

blessed him. Nan prayed earnestly, searching for an answer. She wasn't so much afraid of dying as she was facing the reality of her wasted life and guilt about things going to be left undone and not accomplished. She remembered back when she learned of the first report of the doctors when they said she might have a blood disease. How as she lay in her hospital bed at that time feeling sorry for herself when her minister and his wife came in to have prayer with her. She asked him, "Why me?" He looked right into her eyes and said, "Why not you?"

This was the jolt she needed to get her out of herself. How selfish could she be? Thank God for a man of the Word who is not afraid to speak the truth in love. This seemed to relieve her mind as she kept saying over and over again to herself as she fell asleep, "Why not me?"

Many times over the next few months Nan kept remembering the following Scripture,

... a thorn in the flesh, ... For this thing I besought the Lord thrice, that it might depart from me. And he said unto me, My grace is sufficient for thee: for my strength is made perfect in weakness. Most gladly therefore will I rather glory in my infirmities, that the power of Christ may rest upon me. (2 Corinthians 12:7-9)

Even though Nan had hoped for a cure for the disease, or recovery for her own illness, she accepted it as God's will for her. The main thought was to glorify Him in every situation. She knew if

CHAPTER 5: SEPARATION

she tried false hope in expecting a cure, then she could not be truthful with God and her feelings, so she accepted hope in death. After all, living with the King would be glorious. Her positive attitude toward death and the beautiful testimony she lived, strengthened her husband through the illness and on through the time that Nan finally did transfer from the church universal to the church triumphant. Her strength in God and the power of the Holy Spirit in her life led her husband into a closer walk with Him and now he in turn is helping others to know the strength of this power.

Now unto him that is able to do exceeding abundantly above all that we ask or think, according to the power that worketh in us, Unto him be glory in the church by Christ Jesus throughout all ages, world without end. Amen. (Ephesians 3:20-21)

There are many hurts and pains experienced by separation. One such hurt is brought about because a couple having been married in one church denomination, later on one of the partners wants to join another church group. This was the situation with Tony and Jill.

My family and I were vacationing for a month out west one year and we were staying at a lodge at Lake Tahoe. We were all playing around the swimming pool, laughing and cutting up. Finally, the children started swimming and racing each other in the water and we knew we could not keep up so we excused ourselves. While sitting on the side of the pool, we were discussing our church

HURTING AND HEALING

back home. Even though you are miles away from it, your flock is ever in your thoughts and prayers. As we were talking, a man came over and said he noticed we were talking about church and asked if Page were a minister. Learning that Page was a minister, be began telling us about his background and the problem he was now facing. He and his wife had met at church and fell in love and were married. Everything went well for about seven years. They had two children, he was a good provider and his wife was a loving homemaker; but the problem was that she was now interested in another group outside the church. This religious group was much different from their own church background which began creating conflicts in their home. His question was, "What can I do?"

We explained to him that this was a common problem that many couples experience, even after having been active in their church for many years, going every time the doors were open. "Going to church does not make a person spiritual," we commented. We told him that it is a personal relationship to Jesus Christ that determines a person's piety and His Spirit working in a person's life which gives him Spiritual growth. We told him about couples we had talked with who, after facing a crisis, confessed to us that they had "played church" all these years—that Christ had not been the head and center of their home like they had made others believe that He was. We asked this young man to begin opening up to his wife by being perfectly honest with her and especially open to God's will in his life. We believe that if two people

CHAPTER 5: SEPARATION

are honestly seeking God's will and not their own, that He will guide them into one church in which they can both be happy and inspired to a closer walk with the Lord. The big breakdown in a situation like this is selfishness. Which one is selfish? More than likely, both are selfish, wanting their own way, rather than God's way.

"Until you both come under the Lordship of Christ," I said, "you will continue to have this conflict in worship." We went on to tell him about another concept in the matter which deals with the fact that the woman must come under the authority of her husband, as unto the Lord. The pain on his face began to lessen when he heard us say that it was very important that he be the one to take the initiative and first of all place himself under the complete authority of the Lord Jesus Christ. There will not be separation in your place of worship, we assured him, if you both earnestly pray for God's will in your life. "God will answer your prayers and bless you," I said, "and you will have union in your marriage and worship and communion with God and each other."

In this chapter we have been discussing the hurt that comes from separation, whatever that separation may be. King David was suffering the pain of separation from his Lord after his sin of adultery and murder, and in his heartfelt prayer, inspired by the Holy Spirit, exclaimed,

> *"The sacrifices of God are a broken spirit; a broken and contrite heart, 0 God, thou wilt not despise" (Psalm 51:17 KJV).*

HURTING AND HEALING

And so the beginning of the healing process of any separation that has filled our hearts with pain, is simply a spirit of humility before God.

CHAPTER SIX

EXPECTATION

Be Not Wise in Thine Own Eyes
(Proverbs 3:7)

We are hurt more by our expectations of others than what others actually do to us. This is attributed to the perfectionist attitude.

What I want to bring out in this chapter is a special way in which many of us get hurt. We get hurt, not so much by what people say or do to us, as it is by what we EXPECT people to do for us. In other words, we expect people to act according to our wishes and when they don't measure up, we get hurt.

Not long ago my husband had an experience with one of our members of our congregation that illustrates what I am wanting to show in this particular chapter. An elderly lady had her daughter call Page one evening and ask him if he would have prayer for her over the phone because she was sick with the flu and felt that prayer would be a great help to her. Page did have prayer with her and asked God to heal her and help her and then thanked God in advance for answering the prayer. Page was unable to see the lady for a few weeks after he had prayed with her for various reasons, one was simply not catching her at home when he went by to visit. When he did finally get by to see

HURTING AND HEALING

her, he found her angry and hurt with him. She told him that she was never going back to that church again. He got her to talk about it a little bit and discovered the reason she was hurt was because he did not call her back the next day to check on her to see how she was getting along. She expected him to call, and when he didn't do what she expected, she interpreted it to mean that he did not think that her illness was very serious, or that he did not care. Page expressed his regrets, apologized, and asked her to forgive him. She did not indicate at the time that she would forgive him for not coming up to her expectation, and after several months, she kept her promise of not coming back to church. During the brief visit that Page had with this lady, she relayed to him an experience she had some seventy years before of someone who had hurt her. It is sad to think that in almost all of her eighty years of living, she has been super-sensitive to hurt due to her own expectations, which has caused her to come to the twilight years of her life without friends and the fellowship of the church.

Newlyweds, Tris and Nate, were at a party. Nate went to get his wife some punch, and while he was gone, a married fellow came up to Tris, and out of the clear blue, started making passes toward her. She was humiliated. When Nate came back on the scene with the punch, he stood there chatting, but was unaware and inattentive to his wife's needs as she tried to cope with this flirtatious Romeo. After the party, while they were driving home, Tris was silent and feeling humiliated. Nate, finally, sensing that something was wrong, asked, "Honey, is

CHAPTER 6: EXPECTATION

anything wrong?"

"I'm so angry and upset at that big lug trying to make passes at me at the party," she whined.

Nate replied, "Ah, the guy's got a problem, just forget it."

"That's not why I'm so hurt and humiliated," she retorted. "I'm hurt because I expected you to protect me. You just stood there and let the guy get by with it. You should have put him in his place." Nate was stunned and was quiet for a few minutes as he thought over what she had just said.

"You know darling, you're right. Will you forgive me for not protecting you? I'm new at this and I will have to learn how to protect you in the future. I appreciate your sharing this with me."

This is an unusual situation in which the young man took responsibility for his failure and was able to reconcile the relationship to his bride by realizing that her hurt was a legitimate one, because he should have indeed protected his wife and he did not.

As my husband pointed out in his book, <u>DO YOURSELF A FAVOR: LOVE YOUR WIFE,</u> the husband becomes the spiritual leader according to God's Divine Plan and as a result takes on the roles of Prophet, Priest and King. In the role as King he provides for his queen many things, one of which is PROTECTION.

HURTING AND HEALING

However, there are many more instances in which the reverse of the above story is true, where people "expect" other people to do things for them that are beyond their control. Let me illustrate.

Mrs. Park lived all alone. She was wealthy and she had friends who were very good to her. She had a few relatives and two granddaughters that lived close to her in the same town. Mrs. Park was almost always expecting the granddaughters to do things for her, and when they didn't or couldn't, she would get hurt and mad at them and cause them to go through agony. Because of her selfish attitude of wanting them to do for her now that she was old, she actually drove the granddaughters further away from her.

It is truly sad when people become old and feel like they have done their share and now it is their families or friends turn to do for them. This is an immature attitude. Older people need to continue to do for themselves as long as they possibly can. It is almost dehumanizing them when we do everything for them and take away their effort to get things done. I always felt like part of the fun of doing things in life was the effort you had to put forth to get them accomplished. It is so sad to see a family where Grandma expects everyone in the family to revolve around her because she is old. The older we become, the wiser and more mature we need to be. It is a shame for them to use age as a weapon for meeting their expectations of people in doing things for them.

CHAPTER 6: EXPECTATION

Once I worked in a nursing home and we found that the patients who were encouraged to do things for themselves were a lot happier, had more self-esteem, and adjusted to their environment much easier than those who expected someone to do everything for them. Even people who were confined to wheelchairs, etc., were being taught to take certain responsibilities that they could handle and, needless to say, these people felt better about themselves and were the ones that were not as depressed.

Aunt Lil had lived her life. She was now 80 years old. She had gone through three husbands. She had had money and she lost money. She had her children, his children and their children. She had a lovely home, all the money she needed, and friends. She was struggling in her Christian life to get to know God in a more personal way. However, in her old sin nature she would keep the children always in upheaval, talking about one, then the other, and misquoting things they said or didn't say. She always wanted the children to revolve around her and if one didn't call or come by in a day or so she would always have some smart remark or dig to make to them. When you did go see Aunt Lil she was always complaining and fussing; it sure wasn't a joy to go there. You could tell she had an inner anger because she would put you down or people in the family down. You could tell the jealousy she showed if she didn't get all the attention. She was always in self-pity and hurt. Her main problem was always wanting or expecting her children to do for her and when

HURTING AND HEALING

they didn't, she would get hurt. Her children would call her on the phone from time to time and this is how the conversation would go.

"Hi, Mom, sure is a pretty day."

"Not, really, it's a little chilly over here."

"Say, did you see that good movie on TV last night?"

"No, I can't get many stations on my set."

"Have you heard from your brother lately?"

"No, he never calls, I guess he's too busy. Nobody ever calls me. I don't go anywhere. There's just not much reason to live. Say, would you come over and fix that "salad" for me?"

"Gee, I'd love to, but the baby is sleeping now. You go ahead and make it, I know you can do it."

"Well, I'd rather have you do it, you make it so well."

"Now listen, you go into the kitchen and make it. You need to do more for yourself. You have so much time on your hands, you need to keep busy and so if you make that salad, it will be good for you and give you something to do."

On and on they go, Aunt Lil trying to get everything done for her and daughter trying to get her to do for herself.

CHAPTER 6: EXPECTATION

Aunt Lil gets hurt because she thinks because she is old they should do for her. Her children get upset because they feel she should do for herself the things she can do and give her more reason for living. By the way, every time the daughter hangs up this is how Aunt Lil ends the phone conversation.

"Well, when you aren't too busy, come and see me, there's not much to live for, no one ever comes anymore."

How sad! I wish we had a good education program for "Growing Old Gracefully." Now this isn't to say all older people are like Aunt Lil. Far from it. But I wanted to use this illustration to help you understand why we get hurt when we expect other people to do things for us and they don't come through with our expectations. So many times we are more hurt by what we expect people to do for us than what people actually do to hurt us.

This same thing happens in Church groups. People expect Christians to act a certain way and when they don't measure up, they get hurt.

This happens to ministers more often than not. It is not what the minister says or does that hurts people, as much as what the people expect of him and he doesn't do. He is not measuring up to their expectations.

For example, one day a lady actually raked her minister over the coals for not attending a church "Easter Egg Hunt." She said he should have

HURTING AND HEALING

been there, that he was the head of the church and he should attend everything that goes on at the church. On and on she went. He just shook his head in surprise and asked her to forgive him. Later that night he relayed the information to his wife. His wife asked him why he didn't go the egg hunt. He said he felt like the Sunday school teachers had it under control and furthermore, they had not asked his opinion as to whether they should have it or not, and he felt that church should be the place where children learn the "real meaning of Easter" and not the commercial way. But he said the main reason he didn't go was because one of the members had asked him to stop by his home. While he was there the member had a heart attack and he had stayed there until the emergency squad arrived to take him to the hospital. He said he would convey his thoughts to the Sunday school committee if they wanted them, but felt like the lady who called him down about the occasion had over-reacted, so that she wouldn't have heard him if he did explain why he was not there.

We had one family in one of the churches we served that expected us to be at every occasion that their family had. They had eight children and they were always having birthday parties, weddings, showers, family reunions, and the like. It would have been a full-time job just attending one family's activities and would have not left time for the rest of our flock. They were often hurt with us because they could not understand why we could not always be at their functions. Their hurt was caused not so much by what we did to them, but

CHAPTER 6: EXPECTATION

what they expected us to do for them.

So the next time you are hurt by what you expect someone to do for you, ask yourself—"is that their responsibility, or did I just think they should have done that for me?"

Another hurt is expecting people to be able to read your mind. Many times husband & wife get angry because they are expecting the other to "read their mind." It is like a wife wanting something extra special for Christmas or her birthday. She mentions it months in advance and then expects her husband to pick up on it and get it. So the day of the special occasion arrives and she doesn't get what she had hinted for and so she gets upset and bursts into tears. Her husband doesn't know what's going on. Maybe she will confront him and he will reply, "I don't remember you saying anything about that", or "It completely slipped my mind", or "I wish you would have come right out and told me that's what you wanted. I was racking my brain trying to figure out what to get you!"

Expectations can be little things. I started wearing glasses recently so I could read better. I haven't quite gotten used to the idea of wearing them. They really bother me, except when I'm reading. Consequently, I don't always carry them with me. The other day my daughter and I went shopping. We encountered a large "bargain table." I was picking up different articles and asking my daughter, "How much is this?" "What's the price on this?" After a few articles my

HURTING AND HEALING

daughter asked in an irritated voice, "Mother, where are your glasses?" I felt hurt. I didn't ask her anymore. As we were driving home, I was praying silently about my hurt. I then said to my daughter, "You know, I felt hurt back there in the department store when you asked me where my glasses were. I feel like you didn't want to help me. Plythe responded, "Mom, it's not that I didn't want to help you, it's just that you always ask me to be your eyes for you. Every time we go shopping or to a restaurant, you never have your glasses." Well, when she put it that way, I realized I was asking her to be "responsible" for something that was my responsibility. In other words, we get hurt when we expect other people to take on our responsibility for us and they chose not to do so.

Having expectations in organizations can be hazardous as well. A friend of mine was a member of the Garden Club. She was so excited that they were going to elect officers and she expected to be elected the Publicity Chairman. The morning after the meeting I called to see how the election went. She was so hurt and disappointed because she did not get elected to the position. I asked her if she had expressed to anyone that she wanted that particular job, and that she had a journalism and advertising background. To my surprise, she told me that she just assumed that they knew that and so did not mention it to anyone. So, I tried to explain to her that she could have avoided the hurt if she had taken the responsibility to let the ladies know what she was capable of doing. They simply could not read her mind, and did not know

CHAPTER 6: EXPECTATION

her well enough to know her talents and interests. Now, had they had the information and still not chosen her to that position, then she could have chosen to be hurt or not.

So, please the next time you are hurt because you didn't receive an honor, or get elected, ask yourself if you had assumed all your responsibilities in the matter. Never blame other people for neglecting your own responsibilities. So be not wise in your own eyes, expecting people to meet your expectations, but listen to the Spirit of God and follow His guidance into your relationships and experiences.

CHAPTER SEVEN

FAILURE

He Will Not Fail Thee (Deuteronomy 31:6)

This chapter examines failure, which in essence is Faith in reverse. One must learn to not blame others for one's own mistakes or misfortune.

As I picked up the paper and read the headlines, I couldn't believe what I was reading. "Student Kills College Professor." It seems as though this young man had taken his exams and when he was called in by his college professor to explain that he had failed the exam, the young man took out a gun and shot the professor and then turned the gun to his own head and killed himself.

If this young man could have only seen "failure" in reverse. If he could have blamed himself for his not passing the exam. Failure can prepare a man or woman for a better job ahead. Failure can stop one from going in the direction one is going, which is often selfishness, and cause one to turn to God and ask for His will in one's life. Again, let me emphasize that hurt, pain, and suffering are all allowed by God to strengthen us and to get our attention so that we will become dependent on Him for His plan for our life.

HURTING AND HEALING

WHAT MAY SEEM LIKE FAILURE IN OUR SIGHT, MAY BE SUCCESS IN GOD'S SIGHT!

A friend of mine, Mina, told how it is to be high in one minute with success, and the next minute be at rock bottom. It seems as though when her son, Ben, was a younger lad, he played on a Little League baseball team. One evening, Ben's team was winning the last inning of the game, when Ben hit the ball and was able to go around all three bases and thus, hit a home run. His team won the ball game. What thrill! What joy! What excitement these parents and their son felt as they drove home from the game that evening. They felt like they were really on cloud nine. Ben was the hero of the game. The crisis came shortly after they had tucked Ben into bed—still chattering away as they slipped out the door of the room. The phone rang! It was the Little League official who was calling to say that the game would have to be played over again. He said that young Ben had not touched third base. There it was—mountain top experience, then, bang—the valley! This was so hard for these parents, to go back into Ben's room and tell him the news. All three sat crying and trying hard to console each other.

It is ironic that as I getting the material for writing this chapter, we were going through some thoughts of failure in our own home. Our teen-age daughter, Plythe, came home and announced that she had been chosen from her homeroom class to be a "Homecoming Representative." I was so excited and thrilled since she was a new student at the

CHAPTER 7: FAILURE

high school and knew so few of her classmates there. A representative was chosen from each homeroom and then the whole school would vote for four girls out of eight. I knew that Plythe was aware of what it was like to be a winner, since she had tried out for majorette at her former school and had won that honor. However, I was afraid she didn't quite know how to cope with "failure." So I felt it was my duty as a loving mother to help her work through the "hurt" of not getting Homecoming Representative if she didn't make it. I asked her to think about the worst thing that could happen to her if she didn't get the honor. She thought about it for a minute, and as her big brown eyes looked up at me she replied, "It's not a big deal. I guess about the worst thing that could happen is that I just wouldn't get Homecoming Representative, which I already don't have!" We both realized then that what she already had, in and of herself, was already fine and if she got it, it would be a nice honor, but if she didn't, it would not "hurt" her in any way. A friend of mine asked me how I was going to handle it if Plythe didn't get it, and I replied, "It will give me a good illustration for the book I'm writing." By the way, she didn't get "it" and she handled it like a real trooper. She felt honored just to have been nominated.

In the 16th Chapter of Acts, we learn about how Paul and Silas were put into jail. These men did not see this as "failure" as you and I would have, but they thanked God and sang and prayed. They took this opportunity for relating their message to the other prisoners. They could have sat around feeling sorry for themselves and angry with God. But they chose to believe God would work in every situation for good, because they loved Him and were obedient to Him.

Many people who are "inventors" have had to work in the midst of discouragements, and so-called "failures." They not only had to endure the misunderstanding and criticism, which no doubt drained their strength, but caused a delay in their accomplishments.

Since our son was five years old, he has had a desire to be a medical doctor. His "Grano" made him a little white "Dr. Kildare" doctor's jacket. He kept this his dream through high school, and in the process graduated with "honors." Then came college. Although he still had the dream—he wavered. He wanted a balanced life between bookworm and social life. Because of wavering in his goal, his grades were not the 4.0 average that he needed to get into medical school, and instead he had a 3.5 GPA. Some medical schools would accept a GPA of 3.0, but looked more favorably on the MCAT scores. Perry did not set any records on his MCAT either. When he dressed up in this blue, three-piece suit to take the interview with The Pre-med Committee, he was shocked to learn that they were discouraging him concerning going further into the field of medicine. He was crushed! He graduated and didn't feel the thrill of graduation because three people said that he would not be able to make it in medical school, and

CHAPTER 7: FAILURE

that he should try another field. He came home that summer, feeling dejected and a sense of "failure." We talked and prayed and talked and prayed. I finally said, "I wouldn't let three people be in charge of my destiny." With that remark, he was re-motivated to do something. He started applying to various schools and was soon accepted into the American University of the Caribbean. He is now a licensed Family Practice Medical Doctor in the states of Florida and Michigan. Because of a lot of prayer and being able to swing into plan "B" and "C" and sometimes plan "D", he was able to overcome what seemed to be a failure on his part.

His hurt, SURRENDERED to God, became a hope SUPPLIED. Recently, in talking with him he confessed, "I blamed that Committee for my failure, but when I admitted to God and myself that I was lazy, (I couldn't admit that I was dumb), I was able to take responsibility for my actions and change the direction of my life." When we blame others for our failures, we cannot change, nor grow. But when we accept responsibility for our actions, we can indeed change. Praise the Lord! This power to change comes through prayer and leaving our lives up to God and His will for our life.

REMEMBER, FAILURE IS ONLY TEMPORARY, IF WE LET IT BE!!

In the book of Proverbs we find this bit of wisdom, "A prudent man forseeth the evil, and hideth himself; but the simple pass on, and are punished." (Proverbs 27:12 KJV).

HURTING AND HEALING

So much of the failure we experience in life has to do with our not "winding things out." I can remember when our son was small, he would swing very high on his gym set. I would ask him not to swing so high. He didn't always obey. I then would take him aside—get good eye contact, touch his shoulder, and give him the worst case scenario. "Now, Perry," I would say, "I know swinging high on the swing feels good to you, but at the height you are swinging and rate of speed, should you fall out of the swing, you would crack your head open and Mother would have to rush you to the hospital to have the doctor sew it up!" It was at this point that he seemed to get my message. He began to understand that I was not a spoil sport mom, but a loving mom, concerned for his safety. As he grew older and wanted to make decisions on his own, I would always ask him to "wind out" the consequences. Now to be sure, he had made mistakes and had failures, but through "watching for problems ahead" we are able to eliminate some of those failures.

We know of a young man who was wounded in Vietnam and lost both legs. As he shared with us his experience of his legs being blown off, he said that he never did lose consciousness. I asked what his first thoughts were. He said that he looked down and his first thought was a humorous one, "I've never seen what the inside of my legs looked like before," he replied. "My next thought was that I would never allow this incident to hinder my goals in life," he continued. His response was a good one because he has a very personal relationship with

CHAPTER 7: FAILURE

God, and it was this that helped him stay out of self-pity. He is now with the United States government in a very high office.

Many people, such as Paul, who had the thorn in his flesh; and Fanny Crosby and Helen Keller in their darkness of sight but not of soul—have refused to let "failure" or handicaps become a defeat in their lives.

My husband and I have seen many marriages on the rocks, couples who admitted failures in their marriages, and yet they were willing to change. These changes, brought about by their willingness to listen to God and His Word, have ended up being a real BLESSING to others. That is the way God works.

Sometimes failure, rather than success, prepares a person for a task which he would not have been prepared for if he had not had the failure to learn how to cope and overcome. Oswald Chambers writes: "Why shouldn't we go through heartbreaks? If through a broken heart God can bring His purposes to pass in the world, then thank Him for breaking your heart."

WHEN ONE FAILS IN LIFE, IT DOES NOT CHANGE ONE'S INTRINSIC VALUE! ONE IS NOT A FAILURE—IT SIMPLY MEANS THAT ONE HAS FAILED IN SOME ASPECT OF ONE'S LIFE.

CONCLUSION

Emotional scars from hurt are a terrific burden. However, God can absorb our pain if we simply choose to open our hearts and minds and allow Him in.

Some time ago our family was touring and viewing the newly opened Lawnwood Medical Center. It was a new and important achievement for our town. The medical facility was three stories high and they were having "Open House" for the citizens to go through and see all the modern equipment and services they had to offer. We were instructed to climb the three flights of stairs because they were not using the elevators for this occasion. As we were moving down one of the long corridors, walking and talking with some friends of ours who were prominent people in our city, we noticed their youngest child, Mary Beth, had taken off her boots. She had a real cute outfit on, a darling little red dress with high fashion boots, but she was limping along in stocking feet with her boots in her hand. Her parents looked at her the way parents do when they are questioning what their children are doing, yet without a word. She knew their thoughts and exclaimed, "My feet HURT, these boots are rubbing blisters on my feet!"

As I thought about this little incident, it made me think that life is similar to this. If your feet hurt, you can remove the shoes and relieve the pressure, although the blisters remain. This is true for life as well. When your heart hurts, and has

HURTING AND HEALING

what feels like blisters, the pressure can be removed by a simple act of confessing the hurt to God and to the person who inflicted the hurt. You can then forgive the person and ask forgiveness for yourself to God for any bad feelings you may have had toward the person.

This is like taking off the boots that cause the pressure on your heart. Then, through discipline, you can train your mind to think of something pleasant. The scars will still be on your heart, but the hurt will go away because you have decided to release the pressure. There is a Scripture that, if followed, will provide a habit of a happy life that helps those HURTS:

> "Finally, brethren, whatsoever things are true, whatsoever things are honest, whatsoever things are just, whatsoever things are pure, whatsoever things are lovely, whatsoever things are of good report; if there be any virtue, and if there be any praise, think on these things." (Philippians 4:8).

REFERENCES

Backus, William and Marie Chapian. <u>Why Do I Do What I Don't Want to Do</u>? Minneapolis: Bethany House Publishers, 1984.

Bittner, Vernon J. <u>Make Your Illness Count</u>. Minneapolis: Publishing House, 1976.

Bright, Bill. <u>A Handbook For Christian Maturity</u>. San Bernardino: Campus Crusade for Christ International, 1982.

Collins, Gary. <u>Overcoming Anxiety</u>. Santa Ana: Vision House Publishers, 1973.

Chapman, Elwood N. <u>Your Attitude Is Showing</u>. Chicago: Science Research Associates, Inc., 1987.

Finney, Charles G. <u>Love is not a Special Way of Feeling</u>. Fellowship, Inc. No Date. Minneapolis: Bethany House Publishers

McMillen, S.I. M.D., <u>None of These Diseases</u>. Old Tappan: Revell Company, 1979. Fleming H. Revell Company, 1979

Hendricks, Howard G. <u>Say It With Love</u>. Wheaton: SP Inc., 1973.

Keene, Leonard. <u>Please Don't Hurt Me</u>. Fort Worth: Lindsay Printing, 1975.

HURTING AND HEALING

Lester, Andrew D. <u>Coping With Your Anger</u>. Philadelphia: The Westminster Press, 1983.

Lewis, C.S. <u>The Problem of Pain.</u> New York: MacMillan, Publishing Co., Inc., 1978.

Littauer, Florence<u>. How To Get Along With Difficult People</u>, Eugene: Harvest House Publishers, 1984.

Maxwell, John C. <u>Your Attitude: Key to Success</u>. San Bernardino: Here's Life Publishers, Inc. 1984.

McDowell, Josh. <u>Evidence For Joy</u>. Waco: Word Books, Publishers, 1984.

Osborne, Cecil. <u>Release From Fear And Anxiety</u>. Waco: Word Books Publisher, 1977

Yancey, Philip. <u>Here Is God When It Hurts</u>. Grand Rapids: Zondervan Publishing House, 1977.

ABOUT THE AUTHOR

Patricia R. Williams is a native of Ft. Pierce, Florida. She attended Stetson University in DeLand, Florida, Columbus College in Columbus, Georgia, the Presbyterian School of Education in Richmond, Virginia, and International Bible Institute and Seminary in Orlando, Florida where she earned her doctorate degree in Ministry and Christian Counseling. She also received an honorary degree, Doctor of Letters, from that institution.

She has been a lecturer, seminar leader, and counselor. She recently retired after 25 years teaching and administering the Women's Program at Indian River State College in Ft. Pierce, Florida. At present she is a grief counselor at Haisely Funeral Home in Ft. Pierce.

Patti is the wife of Dr. H. Page Williams who was Pastor of the Indian River Presbyterian Church in Ft. Pierce, Florida. Dr. Williams went to his home in heaven in 1993.

Dr. Patti R. Williams is listed in Contemporary Authors and is the author of *Husbands, For Wives Only*, *The Perfect Woman's Flaw* and *Hurting and Healing*. Individuals from around the world have been helped by the sage wisdom recorded in these books.

Mrs. Williams has two children, Perry Scott Williams, a medical doctor, who is married to Laura, also a medical doctor in Canton, Ohio and Jacklyn Plythe Freedman, who owns "Treasures of Ft. Pierce" website: www.treasuresoffortpierce.com. Plythe has two children, Taylor Page and Brandon Michael.

www.ingramcontent.com/pod-product-compliance
Lightning Source LLC
LaVergne TN
LVHW051601080426
835510LV00020B/3077